This resource of thoroughly researched and well-written dramas will be a valuable addition to any Bible study or church organization desiring to explore and to learn from the lives of women of the Bible. Using engaging personal monologues, the stories of Biblical women will come alive as each woman shares with the audience her thoughts, emotions, and experiences of her life of faith.

—Cheryl L. Nydam
Bible teacher and retreat speaker

Wanda creates a human interest story within the Biblical narrative to create her characters with a compelling dialogue, which shares a much bigger story and brings it to life.

—Judy Clemons
Retired educator

Wanda brings women of the Bible to life while staying true to the Biblical stories. Her monologues are inspirational, moving, and entertaining. Wanda also provides the performer with helpful information on character development, portrayal, and dramatization.

—Melody MacMillan
Church of Christ, Eureka, California

Wanda Bristow has an incredible gift for making Biblical characters come to life through her narration and performances. I have come to intimately know the women—Esther, Ruth, Naomi, Mary and Martha, Mary Mother of Jesus, and Mary Magdalene—through Wanda's performances for our Women's Bible Study. We were truly blessed.

—Nancy DeRuiter
Christian Reformed Church, Escalon, California

I am honored to share that the Biblical dramas written and portrayed by Wanda Bristow were a great blessing to both our traditional and contemporary congregational services at Calvary Reformed Church in Ripon, California. Wanda was an active member of Calvary Church and a wonderful blessing to our congregation in every way. She has performed four of these dramas in our morning worship services: "Mary Magdalene," "Ruth and Naomi," "Queen Esther," and "Mary and Martha of Bethany." So many people personally expressed to me how blessed they were by these dramas as the Bible characters came alive each morning. Perhaps even more amazing for a very diverse congregation—no concerns were raised about a drama replacing the morning sermon. I pray these Bible portrayals and truths may now be helpful to you and will continue to touch lives and deepen your faith in God.

—Duane Laman
Senior Pastor, Calvary Reformed Church,
Ripon, California (1993–2009)

DAUGHTERS
G*of*OD

Biblical Monologues for Women

WANDA WALLIN BRISTOW

WESTBOW
P R E S S®
A DIVISION OF THOMAS NELSON
& ZONDERVAN

WestBow Press books may be ordered through booksellers or by contacting:

WestBow Press
A Division of Thomas Nelson & Zondervan
1663 Liberty Drive
Bloomington, IN 47403
www.westbowpress.com
844-714-3454

ISBN: 978-1-6642-1321-0 (sc)
ISBN: 978-1-6642-1322-7 (hc)
ISBN: 978-1-6642-1320-3 (e)

Library of Congress Control Number: 2020922893

Print information available on the last page.

WestBow Press rev. date: 4/28/2021

I lovingly dedicate my collection of dramas to my husband of sixty-five years, John Alvin Bristow, who now rests in peace with the Lord. John was always my biggest supporter, my counselor, confidant, lover, and best friend. Without John by my side, my dramas would never have come into being.

I also dedicate this book to my three remarkable children: Linda Ruth, Lisa Marie, and John Mark, along with my daughter-in-law, Maria Elizabeth, and son-in-law, Filippo, who all love and serve Jesus. You children bring me great joy and happiness.

To my grandchildren, Francesca, Madison, Evangeline, Marla, Jesse, and Cristopher, along with my grandsons-in-law, Stephen and Keithan, and great granddaughters, Raegan and Gwendolyn: I love you all! You are the light of my life.

ACKNOWLEDGMENTS

I first of all thank my heavenly Father, my Savior and Lord, Jesus Christ, and Holy Spirit for loving me, leading me, and gifting me to write and perform.

I am thankful for my late husband, John, who believed in me, encouraged me, and supported me in all my endeavors. To my three children, Linda, Lisa, and Johnny: your obedience, love, and devotion to Jesus blesses me. Linda joined me on the road and on the stage, composing and singing songs and playing her guitar to embellish my dramas. Lisa very ably edited this book, and I am so very grateful for her devotion to the project and her professional flair. My son, John, is my rock and the spiritual leader of our family.

To Pastor Duane Laman, I appreciate your trust in the validity of my dramas to bring hearts closer to God, thus allowing me to occupy your pulpit on numerous occasions. To Pastor Peter Unruh and Pastor Bill Hayden, and to the numerous other pastors over the years who also opened their pulpits to me, I appreciate you all.

I want to posthumously thank Dena Boar of Calvary Church in Ripon for urging me to write my first biblical drama. She wanted the story of Mary Magdalene for an Easter brunch and would not take no for an answer.

To Jill Sweet and Cheryl Nydam, you have each in your own way, mentored me, loved me, and affected my life profoundly.

To my Bible Study group of women in the Villages—Gerry, Marilynn, Gwen, Kim, Dee, Betty, and Melody—you are truly my sisters in the Lord. Thank you for sharing your lives with me.

To my dear friend, Teres Ryan, professional photographer, thank you for the cover and several other photographs in this book.

To the women of Calvary Church in Ripon and the Villages Community Chapel in San Jose, I thank each and every one of you for your love and friendship. You have enriched my journey.

FOREWORD

In my ministry as a spiritual director, I have learned that it is profitable at times to look backward before moving forward. As I started looking backward in order to write this foreword, memories arrived out of nowhere. What a pleasure to share some of them with you before you move forward to the contents of the book.

The first time I saw Wanda perform, she was Mary Magdalene and we in the audience were transported back to the garden tomb. As Mary responded to Jesus saying her name out loud, I grasped the impact that being called by name can have on a person's soul! To be known by your name provides a deep sense of belonging.

And the first time I heard Wanda pray out loud, I knew Wanda and I belonged together in some fashion. We were both spiritually clothed with a desire for more of God. So shortly thereafter, I stopped her in the church parking lot and convinced her we could lead a women's retreat for the ladies of our church. By the look in Wanda's eye, I could tell she was all for it. However, Wanda, being a little older and a lot wiser, said she had to talk to John, her husband, because he helped her discern what might be too much for their schedule. Part of our belonging together is that we thrive on the next new challenge God places in front of us. You are holding one of those challenges.

For the retreat I volunteered us for, we needed something to tie our talks together. It was obvious to me we needed a drama. Wanda said she was not acting without me because I had talked her into this. So, I played Mary to her Martha in a two-part drama she wrote for the retreat. What fun we had practicing with John as our audience giving us mostly positive feedback! The drama set the tone for the retreat in which our goal was for the women to share their stories with one another. Through laughter and tears, a deep sense of belonging to God and one another permeated the weekend.

Wanda's portrayal of these women became known in churches in the Bay Area, the Central Valley of California, and throughout the state. Several times I traveled with her to help with the logistics of sound, costume, and retreat committees.

While we were co-teaching an evening women's Bible study, Wanda wrote several of the dramas you will soon read, including "Queen Esther." I witnessed, firsthand, how Wanda diligently researched and rehearsed to the point of being able to step into the character's shoes. When I finally saw Wanda as Esther wearing the elaborate dress and headdress she had designed, I felt as if the queen herself had joined us for the evening.

Wanda and I have had a place of belonging in each other's stories for many years, and for that I have great gratitude. I count it all joy to have been present for the writing and first performance of many of these dramas. As these women of the Bible came to life during our times of teaching, speaking, and leading, we were able to share our sense of belonging with others. What a gift it has been.

As you move forward and read these dramas, you will receive the gift of discovering how eloquently Wanda captures the defining moments in the lives of Eve, Hannah, Naomi, Ruth, Esther, Lady Wisdom, Mary Mother of Jesus, Mary Magdalene, Martha of Bethany and Mary of Bethany. It is these defining moments that remind us that we belong in the overarching narrative of God's story among God's people. Then, as you begin rehearsing these dramas, may your laughter and tears once again bring these women to life in such a profound way that your audiences fully experience the joy, peace, and presence of the Lord!

—Jill Sweet, Doctor of Ministry
Come, Learn, Rest Ministries

Charm is deceptive, and beauty is fleeting;
but a woman who fears the Lord is to be praised,
—Proverbs 31:30

CONTENTS

INTRODUCTION

Every woman in the Bible has a story to tell. Some stories are long, and we have the advantage of absorbing the very fabric of their lives, while some stories are only a sentence or two, and we may only imagine what is left unsaid. In many of the stories, we learn of the women by name, but in many other stories, the women, of no less importance, remain unnamed. However, each woman's story is woven into the rich history of the Old and New Testaments. These women's stories are in the Bible for the purpose of allowing us to hear God's voice, and for teaching and setting examples for us to either follow or avoid. I have learned more truths and lessons from these women of the Bible than I can mention here, and I hope you will do the same.

The Bible does not give all the details of anyone's life, not even Jesus's. In writing these monologues, I never deviate from the written words of the story as told in the Bible. I do, however, flesh in details that are not revealed in scripture, and I carefully strive to keep those details consistent and true to the character as described in the Holy Word.

From Eve we learn not to listen to voices other than God's and not to rashly follow the desires of the flesh. From Ruth and Naomi, we learn how to love the women in our lives and lead them to the Lord by our example. From Hannah we learn to never give up on God and that prayers are answered in God's time, in His way, and for His purpose, not our own. From Esther we learn to step out in faith even when the odds are against us, trusting God with our lives and our futures. From Lady Wisdom we learn that God's wisdom is His Son, Jesus the Christ and Messiah. If we desire wisdom, we must follow in the footsteps of Jesus.

From Mary of Nazareth we learn true obedience to the will of God; we learn to put complete trust in Him. From Mary Magdalene we learn to leave our old lives behind when we find Jesus and follow Him no matter what the consequences may be. From Martha and Mary we learn that we must not let the busyness of life deprive us of spending time with Jesus. We must carve out a time to spend with Him. Jesus said that Mary had chosen what was better. She chose to sit at His feet, worship Him, and anoint Him with the perfume of her time.

My prayer for you is that you will grow spiritually and be blessed as you become each of these women and tell their stories to others.

CHARACTER DEVELOPMENT

In this section I will provide techniques and tips on characterization, memorization, and presentation.

WHAT IS A MONOLOGUE?

Since "mono" means one, and "logue" indicates a specific kind of discourse, a monologue is a speech, play, or drama performed by one character. A monologue is spoken by a single actor who is communicating with an audience.

CHARACTERIZATION

Characterization and memorization go hand in hand. Not until you have completely memorized the script can you completely develop the character in your mind. Only when you are free of concentrating on what word comes next will you be free to concentrate on your delivery; free to concentrate on the emotions of your character; and free to become the woman you are portraying. This will take a lot of practice, but the end result will be rewarding and well worth the time spent.

Become as familiar as possible with the character you are portraying. Immerse yourself in all biblical scriptures regarding this character. Read the scriptures over and over again in different

Bible versions, if possible, to get the feel for the specific woman you plan to portray. For example, you may want to read the King James Version (KJV) or The Message (MSG) as well as the New International Version (NIV).

I also recommend that you research the era in which each woman lived and learn about the region, customs, and society. You can find information on the internet; on Christian websites; and in numerous books, available in libraries, that are written on women of the Bible. Once you have internalized all this information and have begun the memorization process, you will gradually become the character. If you are new to performing, give yourself several months to prepare for your performance.

MEMORIZATION

Now, get yourself ready for the memorization process. Begin by reading the entire monologue over and over aloud, becoming accustomed to the flow of words and the sound of your voice. As you read, begin to emphasize words, noticing the changes in mood from sad to happy, from despair to joy, from confusion to understanding. Put yourself in the character's place; try to think and react as she would. Your goal is to become the character.

You are now ready to begin the memorization process. Don't concentrate on dramatization at this point. Start with a sentence, paragraph, or a small section. Read several sentences and then look away from the script and repeat those sentences over and over again. Continue doing this repeatedly for several minutes. Then put the script aside and go about your day. Several hours later, try to remember and repeat those few sentences. If you are unable to remember it, don't despair. Just go back to the script and repeat the process. It is extremely valuable to take a few minutes at bedtime to practice those sentences, since the brain continues to process information while you sleep. You will be surprised when you awake the next morning at just how much you have retained.

Another tried-and-true way to memorize and prepare yourself to face an audience is to recite your lines before a mirror. Looking at yourself in the mirror as you speak simulates standing in front of a room full of people. Another important step is to stand before a trusted friend or family member and recite your piece. Don't worry if you are frightened or if you stumble. Just have your script in your hand and refer to it. Memorization is a process of repetition. From time to time, perform again before this trusted person and continue to solicit his or her valuable feedback.

Another method of memorization is to type the words of the monologue on four-by-six cards. These cards can be carried in a purse, backpack, coat pocket, briefcase, or tote bag. You can practice with these convenient cards while standing in line, while waiting for someone, or while commuting on a plane, train, or bus. However, never attempt to memorize while driving a vehicle, as this will distract your focus away from the road! The act of typing the dialogue is another aide to memorizing. For me, having small segments of script on cards rather than referring to the entire script in a book provides just the right amount of dialogue to learn at a time. Cards divide the script into manageable sections for memorizing. Plus, you can carry the cards around with you without the fear of losing your book. You may also copy sections of the script on your cell phone or tablet.

As you memorize and learn more of the script, characterization and dramatization will begin to flow. Internalize the woman you are portraying and think as she would think in her particular situation. In your mind, become the woman you are portraying. Show her emotions on your face, in your movements, and in your voice. The tone of voice is to the actor what the color palette is to the painter. Keep in mind that a picture in just one color may be dull and boring to the viewer just as a voice of one tone may be dull and boring to the hearer. Emphasize words—let them be either loud or soft, happy or sad—and let your facial expressions and posture back them up. For instance, sagging shoulders or a drooping head suggest sadness; chest out, shoulders up or arms extended express joy or happiness.

As I have said—and it bears repeating—give yourself at least two or three months to complete the memorization process. We have busy lives, and time can slip away from us.

DRAMATIZATION

I am speaking here of your delivery—how you present the memorized script to the audience. Since you now know who this woman was, what she did, and why she did it, it is your job to believably communicate this to the audience. You must get into the mind of this woman and "be" her. Memorization won't make you the character, and the costume won't make you the character—she must be inside your head. When you step onto that stage, you are that woman. You must show her every emotion on your face, in your tone of voice, and with your body. Practice this in front of a mirror and in front of a trusted person. With the script embedded in your mind, the words will flow from your mouth and the drama will emanate from your heart.

THE SCRIPT

All stage directions in my scripts are written in bold text and enclosed in parentheses. They usually appear on the line just before the action, but in some cases, you will find them included in the dialogue. I give you very few stage directions for movement. You are the lone actor on the stage. As you rehearse, try to find occasions for movement. Just as using one tone of voice can be boring, standing motionless in one place is also monotonous.

Practice turning and lifting an arm, taking several steps to either side, walking across the stage as you speak, sitting in a chair, looking up, and lifting your hands toward heaven, hanging your head in shame or sadness, and so forth. Practice these movements as you rehearse, and they will become automatic when you are on stage.

Most characters in the monologues deliver direct quotes from the Bible. The New International Version of the Bible is used for all quotations within my scripts. Direct quotes from the Bible are enclosed within quotation marks and followed by an endnote number. Endnotes are listed at the end of the book by chapter. I include these endnotes for your convenience. I want you to be familiar with the stories that relate to these quotes. If you completely understand the quote and what the biblical character intended, you will find it much easier to memorize your monologue.

PRODUCTION IDEAS

In this section I will give general recommendations on costumes, properties and staging; more specific information is provided for each monologue.

COSTUMES

Costumes for biblical characters are plain and simple unless the character is a queen or a wealthy woman. If you plan to sew your costume, you will find easy patterns in fabric shops for biblical characters, along with the material for the costume. The pattern will have directions for making several styles of tunics, cloaks, and headdresses for women. You may also have a friend or acquaintance who can make your costumes. By watching biblical movies, you can get an idea of what the women wore in the Old and New Testament stories. Biblical costumes can also be purchased on the internet. Personally, I make my own costumes; this keeps expenses down, and I can choose the colors and styles. Some churches, especially the larger congregations, have drama departments that provide biblical costumes.

Properties (Props)

A property or prop is an item that a character uses to help tell the story. For instance, Eve may carry a walking stick, and Mary Magdalene might carry a basket of herbs and spices as she hurries to the tomb of Jesus. Mary of Bethany might carry a jar or bottle that represents precious ointment for anointing Jesus's feet. Martha of Bethany might be sitting at a table, kneading bread. If you plan to use props, you must use them at some point in your rehearsals so you will be adept in front of an audience and use them in a very natural way.

Staging

Keep staging simple unless you are performing in a church that has the resources to set the stage up for you. Again, because I was traveling to various churches and retreats and many times had no idea what type of stage or acting area I would have, I used no staging. If I needed a small table or chair, I would ask the church in advance to provide it.

Microphones

Depending on the projection potential of your voice, the size of the room, and size of the audience, you may need a microphone. If you are speaking to a small group of people—twenty to twenty-five, for example—in a room with good acoustics, you may not need a microphone. However, if you are speaking even to a small group in a large room, church, sanctuary, or auditorium, you will definitely need a microphone. Most churches have clip-on or over-the-ear microphones that you can use. A stationary or hand-held microphone is not desirable since it impairs your movement.

Eve—Mother of All Living

CHAPTER 1

EVE—MOTHER OF ALL LIVING

(Eve enters and moves to center stage. She looks out over the audience for a moment before she speaks.)

You may not recognize me, but I am Eve, your mother—the mother of all living. You know my story. The whole world has known my story from the beginning of time. I, along with Adam, brought sin and suffering into the world. I am the one who listened to Satan; I am the one who took the fruit to Adam and urged him to eat of it. By disobeying God, we brought suffering and death into your lives as well as our own. I am an old woman now, as old as time itself. I am bent with age and ravaged by time.

You can never possibly feel the weight of my guilt; neither can you know my sorrow. Just imagine you were the one who took Satan's bait. Just imagine you were the one to pass sin on to your children. As I look back on what happened, I ask, "Why ... why ... why?"

(As Eve goes through the questions below, she becomes more and more agitated.)

Why did I listen to the serpent? Why did God put that tree in the garden? Why did God allow Satan into the garden? Why didn't God stop me? Why didn't Adam refuse the fruit? Why didn't God give us a second chance before sending us out of the garden?

(On the last three instances of *why*, Eve is crying out to God. She closes her eyes, lifts her face heavenward, and clenches her fists in desperation.)

Why? Why? Why?
These questions have never ceased to haunt me.

(Eve pauses and walks to one side of the stage to change the mood. She looks off into space for a moment. Then, with a smile on her face and joy in her heart, she turns to the audience and speaks.)

The garden was such a lovely place. There are no words to describe it. Eden was heaven … heaven on earth. Everything was perfection: Our bodies were beautiful, strong, and perfect. Our relationship and love for each other were perfect. Our relationship with God was personal and perfect. But our disobedience destroyed all that perfection.

(Eve's joy now turns to sadness and pain.)

After we sinned, it was difficult for me to believe that God still loved us. He punished us mightily. He pronounced lifelong toil and suffering upon us both—and eventually death. I listened in disbelief as He foretold the pain and bondage womankind would suffer due to sin in the world. At the time, I had no idea what this meant.

God drove us out of the garden and into a fearful, hostile

world—a world for which we were not prepared. In the garden, God had provided everything for us; all our needs were fulfilled. But in the world, we had to depend upon ourselves for survival.

But God showed His love for us by sacrificing two of His beloved animals and making clothes for us from their skins. And He made us a love-filled promise. He told me that my offspring would one day crush the serpent's head. How that delighted me. That hateful serpent would not have the last word after all.[1]

After leaving the garden, I began experiencing the suffering that God had foretold. At certain times, I would become extremely irritable with Adam, and then a flow of blood would issue from my body, causing me pain and discomfort. Then came the day the flow stopped, and I was happy.

But as time went by, I began to have strange feelings. The smell of food in the fire made me sick. My breasts were tender, and I didn't want Adam to touch me. In time, my belly began to swell, and it grew larger and larger. What was happening to me? Then one day, I felt something move within me. Adam and I were frightened. Neither of us knew what was happening.

One evening the pains began—horrible pains in my lower body. I lay on the ground, crying and screaming in agony. At times, the pain became so unbearable that I cried out to God to take my life. I suffered all that night, and just before morning's first light, I had an unstoppable urge to push and bear down, or else I would explode.

Adam was terrified. He never left my side. I held on to him as the pushing urge became more intense. Sweat drenched my hair and body. The last thing I remember as I cried out to God for help was the feeling that some inner force was tearing me apart.

A strange cry brought me from the dark abyss into the sunlight of morning. I couldn't identify the sound. It was not a bird or animal sound, but it was sweet to my ears. Then Adam placed a red, squirming bundle of flesh into my arms. It was a tiny, tiny human. I did not know the words *baby* or *child*, and I cried out in joy, "Oh, Adam, with the help of the Lord, I have brought forth a man."[2]

We called our baby Cain, and I thought in the beginning that he was the promised Redeemer, the one who would crush Satan's head. Then we had a second son, whom we called Abel. Maybe he would grow up to be the Redeemer. But that was not God's plan. Our sons grew into manhood, and oh, how it breaks my heart to say that, through my son Cain's jealousy and hatred, murder came into the world.

When Cain killed Abel, I lost both my sons and almost lost my desire to live. Abel was dead, and God had banished Cain. But God was good, and He gave me another son. I called him Seth. I was certain that he was the Redeemer. But no, I was again mistaken. However, God allowed me to understand that the Redeemer would be none of my many children. The Redeemer would arise from Seth's lineage, but not in my lifetime.

I went to my grave without seeing the promised Redeemer— the Savior who would take God's vengeance on Satan, that liar and deceiver. You have not seen the Redeemer either, but trust and know that He did come. I know of His promises of eternal life. I know of the cross where He sacrificed Himself for my sin, for your sin, and for the sins of all the world. I know that His saving grace reaches in two directions from that cross. It reaches backward, all the way to the Garden of Eden ...

(Eve extends her right arm.)

... cleansing me from my fateful sin. And it reaches forward to you ...

(Eve extends her left arm, her body becoming a cross.)

... and beyond, to all those who shall come after you. Our

Redeemer's shed blood cleanses all who have believed, from creation until the day of judgment.

(Eve lowers her arms. She then delivers this last speech in a loving, entreating, joyful manner.)

Praise God for His undying love and mercy. No one has committed a greater sin than Adam and I committed. If we can be forgiven and redeemed, so can you. We were created in the image of God. So were you! All men and women were created in God's image, equal and in partnership one with another. In Christ, and in Christ alone, we can recover that equality and partnership that was lost in the garden.

Praise God for His redeeming love!
Shalom!

(Eve smiles as she clasps her hands in front of her body, bowing her head and shoulders as she gives the shalom greeting. Then she exits the stage.)

End of drama.

Production Notes and Recommendations

Bible Scriptures

Eve's story and the basis for this drama come from Genesis 1:26–31. See also Genesis 2, 3, and 4.

The Character

From the moment Eve walks onto the stage and begins to tell her story, she shows tremendous emotion. Think of it: She has been blamed and maligned down through the centuries as the one person who caused not only the fall of humankind but also every evil sin that has ever been known. But in the end, she ascends from the depths of despair to the heights of glory, bringing to the audience the hope of redemption and salvation through Jesus Christ, God's only Son.

The Character's Relevance to Our Lives Today

Eve was God's perfect creation, His perfect woman. Eve is the mother of all living human beings, and we carry her DNA. Yet Eve was perfectly human, just as we are. She allowed herself to be enticed by Satan, just as we do. Her story reminds us to ask ourselves this question when making decisions: "What would God have me do?" God had a plan, even before the creation of the world, to redeem humanity through His Son. In Genesis 3:15, God foretold that redemption would come through the lineage of Adam and Eve. Redemption is available to us today through the blood of Jesus Christ, shed on the cross.

Stage Direction

If you are a young woman, you can omit the last two sentences in the first paragraph of the monologue that establish Eve as an old woman. Feel free to move about the stage as you go from one emotion or one subject to another. Even a small movement of your head or body will help change the mood. Avoid eye contact with the audience, which can cause you to lose your train of thought and your characterization. Looking directly over the heads of the audience to the back of the room will give the illusion that you are looking at their faces. Remember to pace yourself, and do not rush. Modulate your voice and facial expressions between sadness, grief, happiness, and joy.

Biblical Setting

The Biblical setting for this drama is the Garden of Eden at the time of creation, and also the outside world to which Adam and Eve were banished by God.

Stage Setting

Setting the stage is not required; however, plants, a backdrop, and other items may be used especially if the church where you are performing has access to these assets.

Properties (Props)

Props are not necessary, but you can be creative if you like. Think of items Eve might carry in her hand. She might possibly have a walking stick. If you carry or use a prop, you must rehearse with it at some point so you are comfortable using it; otherwise, it may be a distraction for you and the audience.

Costume

Since Eve predates biblical times, her costume can be a shift or robe made from faux fur material, denoting the skin of an animal. Or she can wear a basic loose cotton robe in an earth-tone color. You can find faux fur material online or in fabric stores, especially during the Halloween season. You can find more information in the costume section of Production Ideas. Eve can wear flip-flop sandals, or her feet can be bare. Eve's hair can either be covered with a scarf or left hanging loose. Her hair would be long, so you might wear a scarf if your hair is short.

Makeup

Eve would not be wearing makeup. However, for a drama, and particularly with stage lighting, Eve's facial features may need to be accentuated. Start with a neutral facial foundation and add mascara and eyeliner to delineate the eyes. A light and natural lip gloss and cheek blush can be added.

Length or Run Time of Monologue

This monologue is fifteen to twenty minutes long, depending upon your portrayal. Remember: never rush unless the script calls for rapid speech. Pauses are powerful.

Ruth and Naomi—Whether Thou Goest, I Will Go

RUTH AND NAOMI— WHITHER THOU GOEST, I WILL GO

A Drama in Two Acts

ACT 1

NAOMI—CALL ME MARA

(Naomi enters cuddling a baby doll in a blanket. She shows the baby to the audience with great pride.)

This is my grandson, baby Obed. He is the son of Ruth and Boaz. Oh, this child is the greatest blessing of my life. In this baby, God has given back all which He took from me. **(Sadly)** Oh yes … God took my husband and my two sons and left me bitter and empty.

(Naomi speaks with passion.)

I cried out to God, "Why have you taken my dearest loved ones from me? What have I done that you punish me so?"

(Naomi questions the audience.)

But who can comprehend the mind of God? Who can know His mysterious ways? For out of my tragedy, God brought forth endless blessings upon my life!

(Naomi is referring to the baby boy. She kisses and holds the child close before gently placing him in a basket or cradle.)

(Naomi turns with a smile to the audience and begins to tell her story.)

I should introduce myself. I am Naomi of Bethlehem. I suppose I am most well known for my loyal and faithful daughter-in-law, Ruth. But she has long since ceased to be my daughter-in-law, for I now call her beloved daughter. She has been much more to me than husband or sons. Her love and devotion brought me out of a fallow place, restoring my faith. Oh, yes, there was a time when I felt abandoned by God. In fact, I was so angry with God I changed my name from Naomi, which means pleasant, to Mara, which means bitterness. Oh, I was consumed with bitterness!

It all began when my husband, Elimelech, moved our family from Bethlehem to Moab and I lost everything dear to me—home, family, and friends. I begged and pleaded with him to stay in Judah. I cried for days. I prayed day and night that God would change Elimelech's heart and turn him away from this foolish idea. I knew that God was not pleased. We had been commanded by God to stay away from idol-worshiping people. But my husband had made up his mind to leave Judah because of the famine, and he would listen to nothing I had to say. He ordered me to be silent and told me to pack what belongings our donkey could carry and what our sons, Mahlon and Kilion, and

I could carry upon our backs. We then said good-bye to Judah and trudged the hot and dusty road to Moab.

Elimelech was happy in Moab. We had a roof over our heads and food to fill our bellies. But I could not be happy. Everything was so strange, and the people were not friendly. It was difficult to keep the Sabbath and to celebrate our feast days and holy days with no other Jews around us. The idolatrous Moabites had their own feast days and temples where they worshiped gods of wood and stone, even offering human sacrifices to these false gods— babies, children, young women. It was horrible!

Then disaster struck. My husband Elimelech died. I felt that his death was God's punishment for our disobedience in moving to Moab. Our sons, Mahlon and Kilion, had grown into manhood, but neither of them enjoyed good health; they were both weak and sickly. Against my warnings, they each took a Moabite woman as a wife. Mahlon married Ruth, and Killion married Orpah. Oh, they were good girls, but they did not know the Living God, and much to my despair they brought their household idols into our home. I had begged my sons to return to Judah when Elimelech died, but they felt a comfort in Moab where they had grown up and married.

We had been in Moab ten years when disaster once more struck our family. Both my sons died, leaving Ruth and Orpah widows. There we were—three helpless widows with no one to take care of us. We lost our home because property could not be owned by women, and we had no means of support. Had we stayed in Judah and trusted God, He would have provided for us during the famine, and none of this would have happened. I was convinced that our disobedience had brought about the untimely deaths of my husband and sons. I felt abandoned by God. He had not even given me a grandson to carry on our family name. My heart and soul were dry and empty. My life meant nothing now.

I cried out to God for deliverance! Was there no hope for me? No future for me? With nothing left for me in Moab, I decided to return to my people. It would be a harsh and dangerous journey and not at all safe for a woman alone. There were wild animals, evil marauders, the heat of the desert with its scorching winds and burning sands, and the uncertainty of obtaining food, water, and shelter along the way. But I could no longer abide the wasteland in which my soul now wandered, and therefore I prepared to return to Judah.

I kissed Orpah and Ruth and told them to return to their fathers' houses. But they both insisted on going with me. I argued with them and told them they should stay in the land of their birth. But they would not leave me.

So, the three of us bundled up what food and water we could carry and started on the hazardous trip to Judah, a trip which could take us weeks. We could not travel in the heat of the day or in the darkness of night; neither could we travel on the main thoroughfare at times for fear of bodily harm. When we had walked only a short distance, I stopped and begged the girls to return home.

I said to them, "Go back, each of you, to your mother's home. May the Lord show kindness to you, as you have shown to your dead and to me. May the Lord grant that each of you will find rest in the home of another husband."[1]

Then I kissed them, and they wept and said to me, "We will go back with you to your people."[2]

Through my tears, I begged them to return and let me go on alone. We wept and embraced each other, and then finally Orpah said good-bye and left us.

But Ruth clung to me, and I said to her, "Look, your sister-in-law is going back to her people and her gods. Go back with her."[3]

Ruth replied, "Don't urge me to leave you, or turn back from you. Where you go, I will go, and where you stay, I will stay. Your people will be my people and your God my God. Where you die, I will die, and there I will be buried. May the Lord deal with me, be it ever so severely, if anything but death separates you and me."[4]

When I heard these amazing words, I stopped urging her to return, and we set out together on the journey of a lifetime. When at long last we reached Bethlehem, the whole town was astir. What a sight we were! **(Naomi laughs.)** We were weary, worn, dirty, and bedraggled. We were hungry, thirsty, and unable to take another step. The people could not believe their eyes. "Can this be Naomi?" they asked.[5]

I replied, "Do not call me Naomi. Call me Mara because the Almighty has made my life very bitter. I went away full, but the Lord has brought me back empty. Why call me Naomi? The Lord has afflicted me; the Almighty has brought misfortune upon me."[6]

(Naomi pauses and looks up and to the side for a few seconds, as if remembering and contemplating her past life. Then, with a smile, she turns to the audience and speaks.)

But now, looking back upon my life, I can see that God had never abandoned me. God had never brought misfortune upon me. He had been with me, watching over me through every trial and every hardship. And when I could bear no more, when I had nothing left inside me, God once more filled my cup. The Lord God blessed me beyond measure. He blessed me with Ruth, a loyal, loving, and noble daughter. Through Ruth, God gave me back my life and, through Ruth, God once more gave me a son. Blessed be the name of the Lord!

(With these words, Naomi turns, picks up the baby, and delivers the application of her story.)

I beg of you today, never let yourself feel abandoned by God as I once did. No matter what happens, put your hope and trust in God, for God is always at work in your life, and He will never forsake you. Had I known these things, I could have saved myself untold grief. But little did I know in my lifetime that everything that befell me was in God's hands and that He had a purpose for Ruth and for me. He used my misfortune in the land of Moab to bring Ruth to Judah where she would become one more link in the chain that would one day produce the Messiah. The almighty has turned my sorrow into joy, and I cry out in praise to Him:

(Joyfully) "You turned my wailing into dancing; you removed my sackcloth and clothed me with joy, that my heart may sing to you and not be silent. O Lord, my God, I will give you thanks forever."[7]

Praise God for His faithfulness.
Shalom.

(Naomi smiles as she clasps her hands in front of her body, bowing her head and shoulders as she gives the shalom farewell.)

End of Act 1

RUTH AND NAOMI— WHITHER THOU GOEST, I WILL GO

ACT 2

RUTH—YOUR GOD SHALL BE MY GOD

(Ruth enters smiling as she begins to tell her story.)

I was but a young girl when the Elimelech family from Judah moved to our village in Moab. They kept to themselves, never joining in our feast days or festivals as we worshiped and sacrificed to our gods. I learned from the whispering women at the village well that this new family worshiped Yahweh, the God of the Israelites. Yahweh was a jealous God who forbade the worship of other gods made of wood or stone. As I grew older, I became more and more intrigued with this invisible God.

My friend Orpha and I became acquainted with Mahlon and Kilion, the two brothers from Judah. They told us of their God and their Sabbath customs. They also told us stories of their God's chosen people: Abraham, Isaac, Jacob, and Moses. Orpha paid little attention to these stories, but I felt drawn to a God who forbade human sacrifice; one who condemned the selling of young virgins as temple prostitutes; a God who loved and spoke to His people.

My fascination with the One God made it easy to fall in love with Mahlon and marry into his Judean family. And I was delighted when my best friend, Orpha, married Mahlon's brother, Kilion. Even though Naomi did not approve of her sons taking Moabite brides, she accepted us into her home and treated us with gentle respect and dignity, something that was unknown for a mother-in-law to do in our Moabite culture. And as time went by, a bond of love, trust, and friendship grew between us.

With the death of my father-in-law, Elimelech, Naomi became depressed and listless. And when both her sons died, she grew bitter and morbid. Nothing could lift the cloud of darkness that hovered over her. Even in my own grief, I tried to comfort her, for she had become a mother to me. I loved and respected her, and it broke my heart to see her suffering so.

When Naomi decided to return to Judah, I knew I had to go with her. I had no desire to remain alone in Moab. She was my family, she needed me, and I could not bear to lose her. She was the kindest and most loving person I had ever known; and furthermore, she was my only link to the One God. For I had a deep longing—a hunger in my heart—for Yahweh. But I also had a great fear. Would I, a Moabitess, be accepted in Judah by God's Chosen People? For this reason, I cried out to Naomi in the desert, "Your people will be my people and your God my God."[1]

It was harvest time when we arrived in Bethlehem. Judah was strange to me, and the people whispered and stared at me as I passed by, but I felt secure and protected by Naomi. I had put my trust in the One God, and I found refuge under His wings.

We were starving, and we needed food. Naomi explained the custom in Judah that allowed the poor and needy to walk behind the reapers in the fields and pick up any sheaves of grain that were dropped or missed. I went gladly to the fields of wheat and barley, thus protecting my mother, Naomi, from the backbreaking labor.

A man named Boaz owned the field where I gleaned. He noticed me one day, and I found favor in his eyes. He knew of my faithfulness to Naomi and of my obedience to God. He instructed his reapers to leave extra sheaves on the ground for me. He warned the men not to harm me, and he told me to stay close to the other women and to glean in his fields and none other. Though I was but a Moabite woman and did not even have the standing of a servant girl, he invited me to eat the midday meal at his table. All day I gleaned under the hot sun, but my pleasure in the basket full of grain that I presented to Naomi at the end of each day made up for my aching back and blistered hands.

When I told Naomi in whose field I had gleaned, she cried, "Boaz! The Lord bless him. He has not stopped showing his kindness to the living and the dead. That man is our close relative; he is one of our Kinsman-Redeemers.[2]

Naomi then explained the kinsman-redeemer law to me. When a man died, the nearest relative or "kinsman" was allowed to "redeem" or purchase the dead man's property and "redeem" or marry the dead man's widow. In fact, it was his duty to do so.

One day, when harvest was nearly over, Naomi said to me, "My daughter, should I not try to find a home for you, where you will be well provided for? Is not Boaz, with whose servant girls you have been working, a kinsman of ours? Tonight, he will be winnowing barley on the threshing floor. Wash and perfume yourself and put on your best clothes. Then go down to the threshing floor, but don't let him know you are there until he has finished eating and drinking. When he lies down, note the place where he is lying. Then go and uncover his feet and lie down. He will tell you what to do."[3]

I trusted Naomi completely and did as she instructed, although I was very frightened. I knew that, according to the law of kinsman-redeemer, I was asking Boaz to marry me by lying at his feet and asking him to spread his coverlet over me. In the middle of the night Boaz awoke and found me lying there, "Who are you?" he asked.[4]

I replied, "I am your servant Ruth. Spread the corner of your garment over me, since you are a kinsman redeemer."[5]

Then Boaz said to me, "The Lord bless you, my daughter. This kindness is greater than that which you showed me earlier; you have not run after the younger men, whether rich or poor. And now, my daughter, don't be afraid. I will do for you all that you ask. All my fellow townsmen know that you are a woman of noble character. Although it is true that I am near of kin, there is a kinsman- redeemer nearer than I. Stay here for the night, and in the morning if he wants to redeem, good; let him redeem. But if he is not willing, as surely as the Lord lives, I will do it. Lie here until morning."[6]

I lay at his feet until morning, rising before daybreak because Boaz had said, "Don't let it be known that a woman came to the threshing floor."[7]

That morning, Boaz went to the town gate and sat until the kinsman-redeemer came along. Boaz spoke to him saying, "Naomi, who has come back from Moab, is selling the piece of land that belonged to our brother Elimelech. I thought I should bring the matter to your attention and suggest that you buy it."[8]

The kinsman readily agreed to buy Elimelech's land, but when he learned that I was part of the bargain, he changed his mind and refused, telling Boaz to buy it himself!

Then Boaz announced to the elders and all the people, "Today you are witnesses that I have bought from Naomi all the property of Elimelich, Kilion and Mahlon. I have also acquired Ruth the Moabitess, Mahlon's widow, as my wife, in order to maintain the name of the dead with his property, so that his name will not disappear from among his family or from the town records. Today you are witnesses!"[9]

Boaz and I were married, and in due time I gave birth to

my first son. I named him Obed, and the women of the city said to Naomi, "Praise be to the Lord, who this day has not left you without a kinsman-redeemer. May he become famous throughout Israel! He will renew your life and sustain you in your old age. For your daughter-in-law, who loves you and who is better to you than seven sons, has given him birth."[10]

Then I sat my son in Naomi's lap, and she cared for him. The women said, "Naomi has a son."[11]

Looking back over my life, I can see God's plan and His hand at work. Through Naomi, the Almighty brought me from the idolatry of Moab into the family of Israel, into the lineage of Boaz, and ultimately into the lineage of the Messiah. My son, Obed, was the father of Jesse, and Jesse was the father of King David. Twenty-eight generations after David, Jesus was born. He came to earth to redeem both Jew and Gentile alike. Is it not fitting that the blood of both Jew and Gentile should be mingled in His veins?

(Ruth now delivers the application of her story.)

Boas was my kinsman-redeemer just as Jesus Christ is your kinsman-redeemer. Just as I was grafted into God's family of Israel through my obedience to the Lord God, you also have been grafted into God's family, the Church, through your obedience to Jesus Christ His Son. I was the bride of Boaz, and likewise, you are the bride of Christ. Just as Boaz paid the price to redeem me, Jesus paid the price to redeem you. Boaz paid that price with coins of silver and gold—but Jesus paid that price with His life's blood.

(Ruth delivers this next speech with exuberance, exultation, energy, and joyfulness.)

In the words of my great-grandson, King David: "I will praise you, O Lord, among the nations; I will sing of you among the peoples. For great is your love, higher than the heavens; Your faithfulness reaches to the skies. Be exalted, O God, above the heavens And let your glory be over all the earth."[12]

(Ruth smiles as she clasps her hands in front of her body, bowing her head and shoulders as she gives the shalom farewell.)

Shalom.

End of drama.

PRODUCTION NOTES AND RECOMMENDATIONS

Bible Scriptures

The Book of Ruth

Ruth and Naomi—A Drama in Two Acts

The book of Ruth is the story of two women whose lives are intertwined. For this reason, I have written two monologues to be performed as one drama. Naomi and Ruth each tells her own story. This drama can be performed by one woman or by two women. I have always performed both women myself, with a song by a soloist or a song by the audience, led by a suitable person, between the acts. An intermission is not advised since the flow and momentum of the drama would be lost.

If one woman is performing both monologues, about five minutes is long enough for a sip of water or hot tea and a costume change. The audience can either enjoy a solo or participate in a song. To make it a quick change, Naomi can wear a long cloak that covers most of her dress. When she removes the cloak and changes the head scarf, Ruth is ready to take the stage. If two women are performing the roles, Ruth will be ready to enter the stage as soon as the singing stops.

The Characters

Naomi

Naomi was an unhappy woman. In Ruth 1:13, Naomi shows her bitterness. She feels that the hand of the Lord is against her and blames God for all her misfortune. In verses 20 and 21, Naomi has actually changed her name from Naomi, which means "my joy" or "pleasant," to Mara, which means "bitter." Naomi was not joyful until the end of the story when Ruth and Boaz had a son. The birth of her grandson gave her a purpose and a future.

It is evident that Naomi had a loving nature toward her daughters-in-law. Why else would Ruth accept God and want to travel with Naomi to Bethlehem, knowing that the Israelites were enemies of Moab? Ruth trusted Naomi and loved her as a mother. Some positive attributes of Naomi in her relationship to Ruth were love, acceptance, wisdom, faithfulness, and strength.

Ruth

In Ruth 3:11, Boaz says to Ruth, "All my fellow townsmen know that you are a woman of noble character." Some of the synonyms for noble are righteous, virtuous, good, honest, uncorrupted, unselfish, brave, and worthy, to name a few. Ruth had all those attributes and more. She was loyal, faithful, and loving to her mother-in-law, Naomi, refusing to abandon her. Ruth was brave as she left her home in Moab and traveled the perilous journey to Israel—a land unknown to her, possibly filled with hostility. Ruth had accepted the one God that Naomi worshiped and vowed to remain with Naomi till death should part them, not knowing what reception she would receive from the Israelites.

Facing starvation, Ruth went alone into the fields to glean sheaves of grain to provide food for the two of them, thus protecting the older woman from the back-breaking labor. The two women shared a deep and loving friendship. Ruth looked upon Naomi as a mother and trusted her with her very life.

CHARACTERS' RELEVANCE TO OUR LIVES TODAY

Naomi

Even though Naomi was an unhappy woman, her faithfulness to God and to her family never wavered. For when her husband moved the family into the forbidden land of Moab, away from God's people, her faith in God remained strong. Even in her great sorrow, she never turned to idol worship. And when her two sons married idol-worshipping Moabite women, she accepted them, grew to love them, and taught them about Yahweh. Naomi was also a woman of strength and courage. When all hope of survival in Moab was lost, she determined to make the treacherous journey alone to her home country of Israel, back to her people and her God. In Naomi we see faithfulness, perseverance, strength of character, integrity, acceptance, and love.

Ruth

Ruth is one of my favorite women in the Bible, and I love to portray her. She is an excellent role model for women and girls. She has strength of character and integrity. Imagine the ridicule and alienation she must have experienced by turning away from the idols of her family and community and turning instead to the strange God of Israel. She was loving and faithful to her mother-in-law, Naomi, and she was brave enough to leave everything she knew and to risk rejection and possible harm at the hands of the Israelites. As Ruth traversed that desolate road from Moab to Israel, she was a woman without a country. But in the end, she knew that she had chosen what was best, for the God of Abraham, Isaac, and Jacob had a plan for her life, and it was good.

The story of Ruth and Naomi contains many themes that are applicable to women of today and have been expanded into Bible studies, books, and movies. Among the many themes in this story are change, survival, loss, hope, faithfulness, friendship, mother-daughter relationship, bonding, and mentoring.

Ruth's words to Naomi in Ruth 1:16–17 from the King James Version, have become two of the most quoted verses in the Bible. In 1954 the song "Whither Thou Goest," written by Guy Singer, topped the music charts. The song was recorded by many artists of that day and was called the wedding song, since it was sung at so many weddings. You can find renditions of it on YouTube.

STAGE DIRECTION

Act 1—Naomi

Naomi enters the stage carrying a doll wrapped in a blanket. She is incredibly happy at this point as she talks about her baby grandson. After laying the baby in a bed or basket, she begins to tell her story of loss, bitterness, and hardship. She can move about the stage as her mood or location changes in the story. Naomi must remember to pick up the baby as she exits the stage at the end of the drama.

Act 2—Ruth

Ruth enters the stage telling her unusual and exciting story. She is free to move about the stage as she goes from one emotion or one subject to another. Even a small movement of the head or body will help change the mood. Avoid eye contact with the audience, which can cause one to lose train of thought and characterization. Looking directly over the heads of the audience to the back of the room will give the illusion of looking at the audience. As Ruth, remember to pace yourself and do not rush. Modulate your voice and facial expressions between sadness, grief, happiness, and joy.

Biblical Setting

The Book of Ruth takes place sometime after the period of the Judges (1375–1050 BC). It is a dark time in Israel's history when people lived to please themselves, not God. Judges 17:6 says, "In those days Israel had no king, everyone did as he saw fit." Israel had turned away from God into idolatry and disobedience.

The Law of Kinsman-Redeemer

In Hebrew law, the kinsman-redeemer was the nearest of kin in a dead man's family. He was expected to marry the destitute widow and purchase her dead husband's property. However, the property remained in the dead man's name, and any sons born to that union would bear the dead man's name. This law kept the dead man's lineage alive. The role of kinsman-redeemer is explained in the book of Ruth and also in Leviticus 25:47–55.

Boaz became Ruth's kinsman-redeemer when he purchased her dead husband's property, thus acquiring her as his wife. The birth of Obed, the son of Boaz and Ruth, redeemed Naomi and her family line, renewing her life and providing her a male protector.

When Ruth went to the threshing floor and asked Boaz to "spread the corner of your garment over me," she was asking him to cover her with his protection, redeem her, and marry her.

Likewise, Christ is our kinsman-redeemer—our spiritual-redeemer. As our spiritual brother, He became our Savior when

He covered us with His blood, paying the price for our redemption with His life, rescuing us from sin and death, and making us (the Church) His bride.

Stage Setting

The stage can be completely bare, or decorated with plants, sheaves of cornstalks, pottery, or baskets. A backdrop can be created suggesting a wheat field, city gate, or town square.

If you have set the stage for Naomi, the same setting can be used for Ruth. If you decide to make changes in the setting between Acts 1 and 2, just remember that you have only five minutes at the most to make the change. Feel free to use your imagination with the settings or have none at all.

Properties (Props)

For Naomi, the baby doll is wrapped in an earth-tone blanket of wool or heavy cotton. A woven basket or small bed on the floor is needed to lay the baby in during the drama. The bed or basket cannot look modern. You can cover either item with a blanket if necessary. Either object should be of earth-tone colors.

For Ruth, props are not needed.

Costumes

Naomi would wear a Hebrew costume. She would have a plain, long dress or robe and possibly a cloak. She would wear sandals, and her hair would be covered by a shawl or cloth.

Ruth's dress may be more elaborate and more colorful than that of Naomi since Ruth's husband, Boaz, was a wealthy landowner and a prominent citizen of Bethlehem. If you are playing both Ruth and Naomi, you may wear the same dress for both characters. Naomi would wear a long cloak to cover Ruth's dress. The cloak would be as long as the dress, sleeveless and loose. You would remove the cloak for the Ruth character.

A scarf or shawl should be used as a headdress to cover the hair of both women. Ruth's could be colorful and Naomi's of earthen tones. This would also differentiate between the two women. (See General Information for details on costumes.)

Makeup

Women in Israel at that time did not wear makeup. However, in a large room and under stage lighting, facial features may need to be accentuated. Start with a neutral facial foundation and add mascara and eyeliner to delineate the eyes. A light and natural lip gloss and cheek blush can be added.

Lengths or Run Time of the Monologue

This performance is fifteen to twenty-five minutes in length for each act. The total performance time is roughly thirty-five to forty minutes.

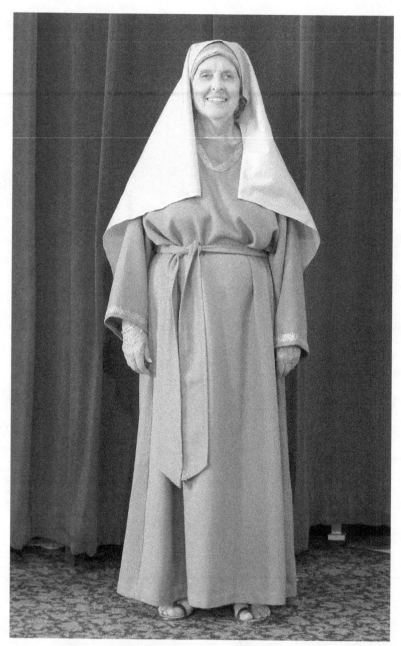

Hannah—The Praying Woman
Photo by Teres Ryan

CHAPTER 3

HANNAH—THE PRAYING WOMAN

(Hannah enters and walks to center stage, looks out over the audience, and greets them with a smile.)

Greetings! I am Hannah, wife of Elkanah the Ephraimite. I am here to tell you my story. I lived in a time when a married woman's worth depended upon her ability to produce sons. I was a young wife who bore the curse of barrenness. I could not even bring forth a daughter for my husband, much less a son. My shame was so great that I could barely hold my head up in the marketplace or at the village well. As time went by and I showed no signs of fertility, it was believed that I had committed a hidden sin that God was holding against me.

My husband had another wife, Peninnah, who was fruitful and bore sons and daughters, one after another. She made my life miserable, taunting me with cruel words and treating me with a superior attitude. Although I knew that my husband loved me, and in many ways showed that I was his favorite wife, my life was filled with sadness and despair.

(Hannah cries out to God in pain and agony from the depths of her heart in this next part of the drama.)

I prayed to God without ceasing that He would open my womb and give me a son. I cried out to God, "Why do you withhold a son from me? What is my sin? I have feared and obeyed you from my childhood. I have kept the law. I have honored and obeyed my husband. O, Lord please, I beg of you, give me a son and take away my shame."

I prayed for years, and I waited, but the Lord was silent. And then the time came for our yearly pilgrimage to the temple of the Lord at Shiloh. There we would offer sacrifices, pray, worship, and celebrate the feast day. While everyone was eating, drinking, and celebrating, I silently stole away from the crowd and entered the temple of the Lord. I stood in the court of the women, weeping and praying silently to the Lord, begging Him for a son. I made a vow to the Lord that day as I prayed: "Oh, Lord Almighty, if you will only look upon your servant's misery and remember me, and not forget your servant but give her a son, then I will give him to the Lord for all the days of his life, and no razor shall ever be used upon his head."[1]

But more shame was heaped upon me when Eli the Priest saw my shoulders shaking as I wept, and my lips moving as I prayed, with no sound coming from my mouth.

He accused me of being drunk, saying to me, "How long will you keep getting drunk? Get rid of your wine."[2]

"Not so, my Lord," I cried. "I am a woman who is deeply troubled. I have not been drinking wine or beer. I was pouring out my soul to the Lord. Do not take your servant for a wicked woman; I have been praying here out of my great anguish and grief."[3]

Eli answered, "Go in peace and may the God of Israel grant you what you have asked of Him."[4]

And I replied, "May your servant find favor in your eyes."[5]

(Hannah shows hopefulness.)

I left the temple that day with hope in my heart, and I returned with my husband, Elkanah, to the hill country of Ephraim. The Lord blessed me and answered my prayers, for I conceived, and in due time I gave birth to a son. How I thanked the Lord for my son, and I praised the Lord, for He had taken away my shame and all reproach against me. I could now hold my head high in the marketplace and at the village well, for at last I was a woman of worth. And because God had answered my ceaseless prayers, I dedicated my son to His service.

I named my son Samuel, which means, "I had asked the Lord for him."[6]

How I loved that baby! I called him Sammy. He had big brown eyes and golden brown curls. When he gave me his toothless grin, drooling with delight, I wondered how I could ever give him up. But I knew I must. I had made a vow unto the Lord.

When Samuel was a little boy and completely weaned, he and I made the journey from our home in the hill country of Ephraim to the temple of the Lord at Shiloh. There he was dedicated to the Lord's service, and I placed him in the hands of Eli the priest.

I had prepared Samuel and myself for this day from the moment of his birth. Although it broke my heart to leave my Sammy, I had made a promise to the Lord which must be honored. God had been faithful to me in giving me a son, and it behooved me to be faithful to Him in return.

On that day as I left the temple alone, I offered up this prayer of praise to the Lord:

(Hannah is exuberant.)

My heart rejoices in the Lord; In the Lord my horn is lifted high; My mouth boasts over my enemies, For I delight in your deliverance. There is no one holy like the Lord; There is no one besides you; There is no rock like our God.[7]

Every year thereafter, I traveled to the temple at Shiloh to sacrifice, worship, and give thanks to the Lord. I was able to visit with Samuel, my son, and each year I took him a new robe that I had lovingly made.

My son, Samuel, continued to grow in stature and in favor with God and with men. As a youth, the Lord called Samuel by name and revealed himself to the boy. When Samuel was grown, God raised him up as a great judge, prophet, and kingmaker in Israel. Oh, but that is another story!

And the Lord God was gracious unto me and blessed me with three more sons and two daughters. For the remainder of my life, I continued to pray for my children and thanked God for His goodness and for His answers to my prayers. Praise be to the Lord, for He is faithful.

(Hannah now delivers the application of her story.)

Through my life and my story, I hope you can see that God answers prayer in His own time—in His own way and for His own purpose. After years of barrenness, despair, and humiliation; after years of humble prayer; after years of waiting on the Lord; the Lord God blessed me with a son. Through so many years of pain and longing, God had prepared me and given me the strength to return my son to Him for His service.

I glorify the Lord in the words of the psalmist David:

(This Psalm is powerful. It sums up Hannah's story. She delivers it with feeling, with joy, with adoration of the Lord who blessed her and turned her life around.)

"I waited patiently for the Lord; He turned to me and heard my cry. He lifted me out of the slimy pit, out of the mud and mire; He set my feet on a rock and gave me a firm place to stand. He put a new song in my mouth, a hymn of praise to our God. Many will see and fear and put their trust in the Lord."[8]

May you, too, be blessed as you fervently pray and learn to wait upon the Lord.

(She smiles as she clasps her hands together in front of her and bows her head and shoulders as she gives this parting word).

And now I bid you shalom.

End of drama.

PRODUCTION NOTES AND RECOMMENDATIONS

Scripture

1 Samuel Chapters 1–3.

The Character

Hannah is a devout, obedient, God-fearing Jewish woman whose life is dominated by her inability to bear a child. In the Hebrew culture of Hannah's day (when judges ruled), a woman's worth and standing in the religious community depended upon her fertility and the bearing of many sons. For years, Hannah prayed to God for a son, but to no avail.

In this drama, Hannah experiences a wide range of emotions in a matter of minutes, from deepest despair to blissful happiness. You must portray these emotions not just with words, but with your heart. Modulate your voice from words spoken in a whisper to words spoken loudly. Hannah cries, she begs, she praises God. Hannah is in the depths of depression and despair when she cries out to God in the temple. Hannah is ecstatically happy when she cries out to God in the second chapter of 1 Samuel. This speech is considered one of the earliest and most stirring poems of the Old Testament. This prayer has been called Hannah's *Magnificat*. The word is Latin and means "my soul magnifies the Lord." Similarly, the Virgin Mary sang a song of praise to the Lord when she encountered Elizabeth in Luke 1:46–55. It is called "Mary's Magnificat" and is also known as the "Song of Mary."

The Character's Relevance to Our Lives Today

Hannah is an example to us of a faithful, praying woman. She never gave up on God. She made a serious promise to God, and she kept it. God had a plan for Samuel's life, and He chose Hannah to accomplish that plan. God needed Samuel to be in the temple under the care of Eli, the priest, when He called the boy to his destiny as one of the greatest prophets in Israel. Through Hannah's obedience to God, He gave her the courage and strength to keep her promise. And in the second chapter of 1 Samuel, as we read Hannah's prayer, we see that God gave her peace in her heart and filled her cup with five more children to love and raise.

What truths can we glean from Hannah's life? Like Hannah, we must be women of prayer, never blaming God for our misfortunes and disappointments. We learn from His Holy Word that God uses our trials and suffering to ultimately bring blessings. God has a plan for each of our lives, and He uses our pain and misfortunes, as He did Hannah's, in fulfilling His plan. Hannah teaches us to pray without ceasing and to never give up on God. She realizes that God always hears our prayers, but answers them in His own time and in His own way and for His own purposes.

Joseph said, in Genesis 50:20, "You intended to harm me, but God intended it for good to accomplish what is now being done, the saving of many lives."

God says through the prophet Isaiah in Isaiah 41:13, "For I am the Lord, your God, who takes hold of your right hand and says to you, do not fear, I will help you."

In John 16:33, Jesus said, "I have told you these things, so that in me you may have peace. In this world you will have trouble. But take heart, I have overcome the world."

Stage Directions

Feel free to move about the stage as you go from one emotion or one subject to another. Even a small movement of your head or body will help change the mood. Avoid eye contact with the audience, which can cause you to lose your place in the drama and your characterization. Looking directly over the audience, just above their heads to the back of the room, will give the illusion that you are looking at them.

Biblical Setting

The Biblical setting for this drama is the hill country of Ephraim in Israel. Samuel became the last of a long line of judges who ruled Israel for over two hundred years. It was Samuel who anointed both Saul and David as king over Israel. God entrusted Samuel to Hannah for his early childhood instruction. At his mother's knee, Samuel learned about the God of heaven and, through Hannah's obedience to God in keeping her promise, Samuel became one of the greatest judges in the history of Israel.

Stage Setting

Potted plants and perhaps a chair or stool for Hannah to sit on, if she wishes, are all that are needed.

Properties (Props)

Props for this drama are optional. Hannah may enter carrying a water jug or a basket, setting it down at the beginning of the drama. As another option, Hannah may carry a baby doll wrapped in a blanket. She may place the baby in a basket before beginning the drama. Depending on the age of the actress playing Hannah, the baby could denote Hannah's child or grandchild.

Costume

Hannah would wear a basic loose robe in an earth tone. She should wear sandals, and her hair should be covered. Dress and headdress styles are discussed in the costume section of Character Portrayals and Production Ideas. Costume ideas for biblical women can be seen on the internet, in biblically historical movies, and in fabric store pattern books. If you wish to purchase a costume, you can find places to purchase biblical costumes online.

Makeup

Women in Israel at that time did not wear makeup. However, in a large room and under stage lighting, Hannah's facial features may need to be accentuated. Start with a neutral facial foundation and add mascara and eyeliner to delineate the eyes. A light and natural lip gloss and cheek blush can be added.

Length of Monologue or Run Time

This monologue is approximately twenty-five to thirty minutes long, depending upon your portrayal. Never rush unless the script calls for rapid speech. Pauses are powerful.

Queen Esther—For Such a Time as This

CHAPTER 4

QUEEN ESTHER—FOR SUCH A TIME AS THIS

(With head held high, Queen Esther makes a regal entrance to center stage. She surveys the audience before she speaks.)

I stand before you as a powerful queen—Queen Esther of the Media-Persian Empire.

(Esther asks the following questions derisively, mimicking those who would challenge her right to be queen.)

You may ask the question, "How could you ever become a queen? You, a woman of humble origin, an exile from a foreign land, and above all, a Jew!"

(Esther resumes her regal stance as she accentuates the following speech.)

My answer to your question is this: "Nothing is impossible with God."

More than one hundred years before I was born, my people—the Children of Israel, the Hebrew nation—turned away from

God to worship idols of wood and stone. God punished them by allowing them to be conquered by King Nebuchadnezzar, who carried them off into Babylonian captivity. Babylon was afterwards conquered by the Medes and then by the Persians, but our captivity continued.

Eventually a king arose who allowed a remnant of the Jews to return to Israel to rebuild the walls of Jerusalem. Those who remained in Persia were allowed the freedom to live in peace; till their own fields and vineyards; tend their own sheep; become merchants and tradesmen; and to privately worship their God without persecution. And after many generations, they knew no other way of life, and few, if any, of the Medes or Persians knew or remembered that they were Jews.

Both my parents died when I was a young child, and I was taken to live with my cousin, Mordecai, who loved me and raised me as his own daughter. He taught me to be honest, trustworthy, and truthful—a person of integrity. And above all, he taught me to worship and serve the God of our Fathers.

In my lifetime, Persia was the largest kingdom in the world with one hundred twenty-seven provinces that reached all the way from India to Egypt. Within these provinces or countries, lived people of different nationalities, speaking different dialects and languages .

Mordecai and I lived in the capitol city of Susa, which surrounded the military citadel and the palace of Xerxes, the Persian king. King Xerxes had a passion for banquets and parties, and after returning from one of his successful military campaigns, he hosted a huge banquet that lasted six months. He invited his generals and wealthy noblemen from all over the kingdom. You cannot imagine the eating, drinking, entertainment, revelry, and orgies that went on. On the last evening of his great party, being quite drunk with wine, King Xerxes commanded his beautiful Queen Vashti to appear before the banquet room of drunken, brawling, brutish men and allow them to look upon her unveiled beauty. But the queen refused to degrade herself in such a manner.

Now, Queen Vashti's refusal—her disobedience—was a public insult to the king, and it could not go unpunished. Xerxes decreed that Vashti should be banished from Susa and from his presence forever. In the following days, he regretted his actions because he loved Vashti. But his decree had been made, and it was a law of the land that a king's decree, once made, could never be reversed or changed. So, beautiful Queen Vashti was exiled, and Xerxes was without a queen.

In due time, the search began for a new queen to replace Vashti. From every province of the kingdom, the most beautiful and purest young virgins were brought to the palace.

(Esther delivers this next speech with fear and building agitation.)

I clung to Mordecai in terror as the king's men pounded on our door. I fought and screamed as I was torn from Mordecai's arms and taken to the palace where I was put into the king's harem along with the hundreds of other girls. I was sick at heart. I could not eat; neither could I sleep. I just wanted to go home to Mordecai.

(Esther takes a few steps to the side to change the mood, then turns and faces the audience and calmly continues.)

Somehow, I soon found favor with Hegai, the king's eunuch, who was in charge of the harem. He gave me special foods, the best room in the harem, and seven maids to wait upon me. We virgins had to complete one whole year of beauty treatments before we could be called in to spend one night with the king. When our name was called, we could choose anything we wanted to wear into the king's presence to enhance our beauty and increase our chance of being chosen queen. We each had our choice of costly gowns embroidered with gold threads; jewelry of gold and precious stones; and exotic adornments for our hair. After one night with the king, we would be transferred to the hall of the concubines, for we would no longer be virgins. And we would most likely never see the king again unless he called for one of us by name.

After my year of preparation, it was, at last, my turn to enter the king's bedchamber. Hegai himself chose my gown and arranged my hair. I had no desire to impress the king with a painted face, costly jewels, or seductive clothing.

After that one night, I was surprised to be called back again and again, not only to the king's bedchamber, but to walk and talk with him in the gardens and dine with him at his table. I was further amazed to learn that I had pleased the king more than any of the other virgins, and that he wanted to make me his queen.

With great pomp and ceremony, I was married to King Xerxes and crowned queen of the Media-Persian Empire. A holiday was declared in my honor throughout the land. A great celebration was prepared that lasted for weeks and included eating, drinking, dancing, and entertainment.

Before I was separated from Mordecai, he had warned me never to reveal that I was a Jew, and as always, I obeyed him. Every day while I was in the harem, Mordecai had walked to and fro near the courtyard, trying to learn how I was and what was happening to me. After I was crowned queen, Mordecai secured a position in the king's service so he could stay nearby. As he sat at the king's gate along with the other city officials, we could easily send messages back and forth to each other.

On one occasion, as Mordecai sat at the king's gate, he overheard two of the royal officials plotting to assassinate the king. Mordecai sent me the message, and I immediately told the king, hoping he would reward Mordecai for uncovering the plot and saving his life. But the king soon forgot Mordecai's faithfulness, and no reward was given.

As time passed, I grew accustomed to life at court. I observed a nobleman at court named Haman, who was power hungry, self-serving, avaricious, and crafty. For some reason unknown to me, King Xerxes elevated Haman higher than all the other nobles. He put his own royal ring upon Haman's finger and made him second in command, or prime minister of the kingdom. The king commanded all the other nobles and officials to bow down and pay honor to Haman.

One day, as my cousin Mordecai served at the king's gate, Haman passed by, and everyone except Mordecai bowed down and paid homage to him. Mordecai's continued refusal to bow down infuriated Haman, and when he learned that Mordecai was a Jew, he plotted to take revenge, not only on Mordecai, but on the entire Jewish nation. For Haman was an Agagite, and his hatred of the Jews went back some five hundred years to the time when King Saul had almost annihilated the Agagite nation in battle.

Haman devised a plan to take his revenge. He had the court astrologers cast the *pur* or dice to decide in which month the execution of Mordecai and the Jews would take place. The pur fell on the thirteenth day of the month of Adar. Haman then approached King Xerxes, telling him that the Jews all over the kingdom had strange customs, were disobedient to the king's laws, and that they should be destroyed. The king believed Haman's lies and signed his request into law saying, "Do with the people as you please." [1]

Haman lost no time in sending dispatches to every corner of the Kingdom, declaring that, on the thirteenth day of the month of Adar, all Jews—men, women, and children of all ages—should be destroyed. They were to be murdered—completely annihilated—and their possessions were to be given to those who killed them.

When Mordecai heard the terrible news, he tore his clothes, put on sackcloth and ashes, and went out into the city, wailing loudly and bitterly. And the cries and wails of the Jews could be heard in every city and province of Persia. When I heard that my beloved Mordecai lay at the gate in sackcloth and ashes, I immediately sent my servant to find out what was happening. Mordecai sent back a copy of the king's decree, of which I knew nothing, and a message that I should enter the king's presence and beg for the lives of my people.

(Esther delivers this next speech with great anguish.)

How could I do this without revealing that I, too, was a Jew? I would be risking my life.

I sent this reply back to Mordecai: "All the kings officials and the people of the royal provinces know that for any man or woman who approaches the king in the inner court without being summoned the king has but one law: that he be put to death. The only exception to this is for the king to extend the gold scepter to him and spare his life. But thirty days have passed since I was called to go to the king."[2]

When my words were repeated to Mordecai, he sent back this answer: "Do not think that because you are in the king's house you alone of all the Jews will escape. For if you remain silent at this time, relief and deliverance for the Jews will arise from another place, but you and your father's family will perish. And who knows but that you have come to royal position for such a time as this?"[3]

"For such a time as this … for such a time as this …" These words cut me to the heart. I sent this message to Mordecai:

(Esther delivers this next speech with great passion and determination.)

"Go, gather together all the Jews who are in Susa, and fast for me. Do not eat or drink for three days, night or day. I and my maids will fast as you do. When this is done, I will go to the King, even though it is against the law. And if I perish, I perish."[4]

(Esther once again speaks as a regal queen.)

On the third day, I put on my royal robes and stood in the inner court of the palace, facing the king's hall. The king was sitting on his royal throne in the hall, facing the inner court. When he saw me standing in the court ... **(She pauses in fearful anticipation, then speaks with relief.)** ... he was pleased with me and held out his golden scepter. I humbly approached the throne, bowing low and touching the tip of the scepter with my hand.

King Xerxes asked, "What is it, Queen Esther? What is your request? Even up to half the Kingdom, it will be given you."[5]

"If it pleases the king," I replied, "Let the king, together with Haman, come today to a banquet I have prepared for him."[6]

Now as you know, the king loved banquets, and Haman was delighted with this honor. As the king and Haman sat drinking wine at my table, enjoying the delicacies provided, King Xerxes again asked me to tell him what I wanted, for he would give me up to half his kingdom. I replied that I would host a similar banquet the next day, and at that time I would give him my petition.

Haman left my table that day a happy and satisfied man; that is, until he passed Mordecai at the gate. Everyone was bowing and obediently acknowledging him, except Mordecai. Haman was enraged.

(Esther mimics Haman's boasting.) When Haman reached home, he called in his closest friends along with his wife and began to boast about his great wealth, his many sons, how the king had honored him above all other nobles and officials, and how he was the only person that Queen Esther had invited to her banquet with the king. **(Esther shows Haman's hatred of Mordecai.)** But all of this wealth and honor was nothing to him as long as Mordecai the Jew sat at the king's gate.

Then his wife and friends said to him, "Have a gallows built, seventy-five feet high, and ask the king in the morning to have Mordecai hanged on it. Then go with the king to the dinner and be happy."[7]

But that night, the king could not sleep, so he ordered the record book of his reign to be brought in and read to him. It was found in the record that Mordecai had saved the king's life when the two guards had conspired to assassinate him. He asked his secretary what honor had been given Mordecai, and the secretary answered, "Nothing has been done for him."[8]

The next morning when Haman came to court to speak to the king about hanging Mordecai, Xerxes called him in to inquire what reward Mordecai deserved.

King Xerxes said to Haman, "What should be done for the man the King delights to honor?"[9]

Thinking the king was speaking of him, Haman suggested that one of the king's royal robes should be put upon the man and he should be seated upon the king's royal horse. A royal prince should lead the horse throughout the streets of the town proclaiming, "This is what is done for the man the King delights to honor!"[10]

"Go at once," the king commanded Haman. "Get the robe and the horse and do just as you have suggested for Mordecai the Jew, who sits at the king's gate. Do not neglect anything you have recommended"[11] You can imagine Haman's indignation and fury!

That very same day, Haman, along with the king, attended my second banquet. Xerxes once again asked me for my petition and for my request.

(Esther delivers this next speech with humility, fear, and earnest supplication.)

I replied, "If I have found favor with you, O king, and if it pleases your Majesty, grant me my life—this is my petition. And spare my people—this is my request. For I and my people have been sold for destruction and slaughter and annihilation. If we had merely been sold as male and female slaves, I would have kept quiet, for no such distress would justify disturbing the king."[12]

With indignation, the king asked, "Who is he? Where is the man who has dared to do such a thing?" [13]

(Esther delivers this next speech with power and fury, accentuating every word.)

I answered, "The adversary and enemy is this vile Haman."[14]

(Esther builds to the climax.) The king jumped up in a rage and went out into the palace garden. Haman was terrified and began shaking and babbling like someone gone mad. He then fell upon the couch where I was reclining and hovered over me like a crazed animal, begging for his life.

At that moment, the king returned to the room and exclaimed, "Will he even molest the Queen while she is with me in the house?"[15] And he immediately ordered Haman hanged on the gallows he had prepared for Mordecai the Jew.

(In a change of pace here, Esther walks across the stage and speaks in a calm voice.)

The deed was done, and that same day Xerxes gave to me the estate of Haman. I appointed my cousin, Mordecai, ruler over the estate, and the king gave Mordecai his own signet ring and made him second in command over the kingdom.

(Esther earnestly pleads for her life and that of her people.)

I then fell at Xerxes' feet, weeping and begging him to save my people. The king's law of destruction could not be changed or rescinded, and men all over the kingdom were waiting for the thirteenth day of Adar on which they were prepared to bring death to my people.

Even though the law could not be changed, King Xerxes told Mordecai and me to write a decree in his name on behalf of the Jews and seal it with his ring. We lost no time in writing a new law stating that, on the thirteenth day of Adar, Jews would be allowed to assemble and protect themselves and kill anyone who might attack them. The scribes were called in, and copies of the law were sent out by couriers on the king's fastest horses to every province in the kingdom.

On the thirteenth day of the month of Adar, the battles began. Five hundred men were killed by the Jews in the city of Susa, including Haman's ten sons, and throughout the kingdom, seventy-five thousand of our enemies were slain. My people had been saved. The day of sorrow had become a day of rejoicing. Mordecai declared the fourteenth and fifteenth days of Adar as feast days and called the holiday Purim— a holiday that has never ceased to be observed every year by Jews, from that day until this.[16]

(Esther now delivers the application of her story; she emphasizes the word *my*.)

My story is now ended, but, my friends, each of you is living out your own story! No matter how small or insignificant you may feel, God has a plan for your life. Never underestimate God's power to use you in a mighty way.

I was only a humble girl leading a simple life, but God used me to save His people. By following God's leading, I was empowered to save the Jewish Nation. For without the Jewish Nation, there would have been no Messiah. And without the Messiah, the world would be lost. Unknown to me in my lifetime, I was one more person used by God to pave the way for the coming of the Christ.

So, I beg of you to listen for God's calling! Be open to God's leading and say, "Use me, Lord." Always remember that God has placed each one of you where you are today "for such a time as this," and you may never know until the other side of eternity what awesome works God did through you.

Praises to our mighty God!

(She smiles as she clasps her hands in front of her body, bowing her head and shoulders as she gives this parting word.)

Shalom!

End of drama.

Production Notes and Recommendations

Scriptures

The Book of Esther

The Character

Esther is a faithful Hebrew woman, obedient to God and to Mordecai. Esther is a master storyteller. She will keep the audience on the edges of their chairs. In order to keep this monologue from becoming monotonous, remember the color palette of the painter. Color your speech with both loud and soft tones and with voice and facial expressions of anger, fear, determination, joy, and triumph. Esther is a powerful woman with a powerful message.

The Character's Relevance to Our Lives Today

Esther is one of the greatest heroines of the Bible. There have been numerous fiction and non-fiction books and Bible study lessons written, as well as several movies made, about Queen Esther. Facing death, she laid her life on the line and saved a nation of people from extinction. Esther is a role model of bravery, courage, and integrity for women and girls.

Stage Direction

From Esther's opening lines, she speaks with authority. She is a queen who is well loved and respected by the king of Persia and who, along with her uncle Mordecai, gained ruling power granted by King Xerxes.

Feel free to move about the stage as you go from one emotion or one subject to another. Even a small movement of your head or body will help change the mood. Avoid eye contact with the audience, which can cause you to lose your train of thought. Looking directly over their heads to the back of the room will give the illusion that you are looking at them.

Biblical Setting

The setting for this monologue is the palace of Ahasuerus Xerxes, who was king of the Persian Empire between 486 and 465 BC. The Children of Israel had been taken into Babylonian captivity by King Nebuchadnezzar many years before Esther's lifetime. When a remnant of the exiles was allowed to return to Jerusalem to rebuild the temple, members of Esther's family line were among the many Jews who chose to remain in Persia.

Xerxes was the most powerful monarch in the world at that time. Persia consisted of 127 provinces (states or small countries) reaching from India to Egypt.

Stage Setting

The setting for this drama can be as plain or as ornate as you wish. I performed at one church that set the stage with artificial ficus trees and potted plants. Church members created a throne using a large fan-backed wicker chair. An ornate chest was spilling out with colorful scarves and other artifacts. A haram or servant girl in costume sat on the floor amid several pillows, playing the tambourine and finger cymbals at appropriate intervals.

Properties (Props)

Esther does not need props since she is basically telling her story. But feel free to use your imagination.

Costume

Since Esther is a Persian queen of the largest empire in the world, she is not dressed in the simple style of Hebrew women, but rather in the Egyptian style of Queen Cleopatra. Her costume can be elaborate with necklaces, rings, dangling earrings, and multiple bracelets. She can wear a flowing headdress or she can wear her hair done up in braids or curls. If no headdress is worn, her hair can be adorned with feathers, ornate pins, a crown, or tiara. I made my own gown for Esther and adorned it with a gold belt and costume jewelry from the 1970s. Costume jewelry can be found in thrift shops or in your grandmother's jewelry box. Esther wears sandals that may be gold or silver, natural leather colors, or a color to match her gown.

Makeup

Esther would be wearing heavy makeup in the Egyptian fashion, similar to that shown in pictures of Cleopatra. She was queen of the largest kingdom in the world and can be lavishly made up. Start with a neutral facial foundation. Heavy eye makeup can include blue, green, or lavender eyeshadow, heavy liner around the eyes, and mascara on eyelashes. Finish with red lipstick and rouge. Fingernails and toenails can even be painted.

Length of Monologue or Run Time

This monologue is approximately thirty to thirty-five minutes long, depending on your portrayal. Remember to never rush unless the script calls for rapid speech. Pauses are powerful.

Lady Wisdom—Listen to My Voice

CHAPTER 5

LADY WISDOM—
LISTEN TO MY VOICE

(Lady Wisdom enters to center stage. She assumes a regal air, looks out over the heads of the audience, and leaves a short pause before beginning to speak.)

Lady Wisdom:

"Listen, for I have worthy things to say; I open my lips to speak what is right. My mouth speaks what is true, for my lips detest wickedness. Choose my instruction instead of silver, knowledge rather than choice gold, for wisdom is more precious than rubies, and nothing you desire can compare with her. I, wisdom dwell together with prudence; I possess knowledge and discretion. To fear the Lord is to hate evil; I hate pride and arrogance, evil behavior and perverse speech."[1]

"The Lord brought me forth as the first of His works, before His deeds of old; I was appointed from eternity, from the beginning, before the world began. When there were no oceans, I was given birth, when there were no springs abounding with water; before the mountains were settled in place, before the hills, I was given birth, before He made the earth or its fields or any of the dust of the world.

"I was there when He set the heavens in place, when He marked out the horizon on the face of the deep, when He established the clouds above and fixed securely the fountains of the deep, when He gave the sea its boundary so the waters would not overstep His command, and when He marked out the foundations of the earth. Then I was the craftsman at His side. I was filled with delight day after day, rejoicing always in His presence, rejoicing in His whole world and delighting in mankind.

"Now then, my children, listen to me; blessed are those who keep my ways. Listen to my instruction and be wise; do not ignore it. Blessed is the person who listens to me, watching daily at my doors, waiting at my doorway. For whoever finds me finds life and receives favor from the Lord. But whoever fails to find me harms themself; all who hate me love death."[2]

(If this is a two-woman presentation, Lady Wisdom turns and regally exits the stage. She does not rush. The Storyteller will immediately enter with an urgency as she admonishes the audience to "Listen and heed Wisdom's call."

If this is a one-woman presentation, the presenter makes the transition from Lady Wisdom to the Storyteller by walking to side stage for an onstage costume change. She places a cape or shawl over her gown and replaces Lady Wisdom's head covering with the Storyteller's hat. She picks up her walking stick and returns to center stage where she faces the audience. She no longer speaks as a regal being, but as a storyteller who has come to bring the Good News of Jesus, who is the Wisdom of God. Her first words are those of urgency as she admonishes the audience to "Listen and heed Wisdom's call.")

Storyteller:

Hark! Listen! The Voice of Lady Wisdom is calling you, daughters of God, sisters of Eve! Do you hear her calling? Can you hear her voice? Give heed to her teaching.

I beg you to listen to Wisdom's voice. Hers is not the voice of man's wisdom—the collective knowledge of the ages, the words of mankind's greatest thinkers and philosophers stored in prestigious halls of learning.

No. Hers is the voice of God's Wisdom—a Wisdom that existed in the Trinity before the creation of the world, before God breathed into Adam's nostrils the breath of life. Some embraced her Wisdom, while others rejected it.

Adam and Eve, the first fruits of God's creation, rejected Wisdom. They chose to listen to the false voice of the evil one, tossing Wisdom to the wind. From that time forward, humankind lost sight of God's Wisdom and sought the pleasures of the flesh rather than the mind of God.

However, a faithful few followed the Living God and refused to worship graven images. They listened for the voice of the Great I Am. Those faithful few bowed in humble obedience before God their creator. They meditated upon Him day and night, they prayed without ceasing, they heard His voice, and they believed His promises. They fell prostrate before Him, crying out, "Thy will be done."

To those faithful few, God sent the Holy Spirit from heaven to fill their hearts and minds with His Wisdom. Through the Holy Spirit, God empowered those who chose to serve Him. Some He empowered to lead His people. To others He gave the gift of prophesy. And He inspired some to bring His words to life on the pages of His Holy Book.

You may ask, "What is this Wisdom? I desire it. Tell me again, how I can obtain it?"

Listen, for this is what the Lord says: "The fear of the Lord is the beginning of knowledge, but fools despise wisdom and discipline."[3]

And again, the Lord says, "Trust in the Lord with all your heart and lean not on your own understanding; in all your ways acknowledged Him, and He will make your paths straight."[4]

But I must tell you, even those who listened for God's voice and obeyed His commands failed. No one could live a sinless life of perfection and Wisdom. No, not one. What more could be expected? After all, they were only human.

God, in His infinite Wisdom, knew before the creation of the world that every human being created in His spiritual likeness would reject Wisdom and fall into sinfulness. From the beginning, God had a plan for their redemption. He planned to send His Son Jesus Christ into the world to save His children from their sins. Jesus Christ was God's Wisdom descending in the flesh, for Jesus said of himself, "And now one greater than Solomon is here."[5]

You ask me how to obtain Wisdom. In the past, God used Lady Wisdom's voice to instruct the people. And then God sent His only Son—the source of all Wisdom—to earth. Jesus Christ is the Wisdom of God. He came to impart His wisdom to all who would believe on Him. He is the great teacher. If you would have Wisdom, you must learn Wisdom from Jesus.

Jesus is the water of life. Drink of His water, and you will never again thirst. To have the Wisdom of Jesus, you must drink from His well.

Jesus is the bread of life. Eat of His bread, and you will never hunger again. To have the Wisdom of Jesus, you must eat of His bread.

Jesus is the light of the world. Walk in His light, and you will no longer live in darkness. To have the Wisdom of Jesus, you must carry His light in your heart.

Jesus is the Word of life. If you live in His Word, you will drink of His water, you will eat of His bread, and you will walk in His light.

Let Jesus—the Word of God—live in you. Let Him be in your heart as you waken in the morning; let Him abide in your thoughts throughout the day; let Him lead your meditations in the evening; let Him cover you like a soft cloud as you peacefully sleep through the night.

My children, if you seek God's Wisdom, you must first seek Christ. To walk daily in the footsteps of Christ is to grow daily in His Wisdom. Without Christ there is no Wisdom, and life has no meaning, no hope, and no future. Without Christ, life is hard and the grave is the only reward.

But when you have Christ, you have God's unfailing promises—promises of His forgiveness, His blessings, His undying love, and His peace that passes understanding. Christ will walk with you and support you through life's darkest days. In Him you have a friend like none other, a friend who will always love you—unconditionally. You have Christ's promise of a happy life in eternity with no pain, no tears, and no sorrow. Christ died on the cross for you. All He asks is that you live for Him.

You may only have glimpses of Christ in this life, but one day you will stand before Him, and you will see Him face to face. My friends, Christ is Wisdom.[6] He stands at the door of your heart and calls your name. Will you listen to Him and answer His call?

I pray for you at this moment that you will choose Christ, have life, and gain Wisdom.

And now, listen to what the Lord says: "Blessed is the person who finds Wisdom, the person who gains understanding, for she is more profitable than silver and yields better returns than gold. She is more precious than rubies; nothing you desire can compare with her. Long life is in her right hand; and in her left are riches and honor. Her ways are pleasant ways and all her paths are peace. She is a tree of life to those who embrace her; those who lay hold of her will be blessed."[7]

(She bows to the audience and exits the stage.)

End of drama.

Production Notes and Recommendations

Bible Scriptures

This drama is based on readings from the book of Proverbs, Psalms, and the New Testament. As you learn this drama, it will be helpful to read Proverbs chapters 1–9. This will give you a clearer understanding of Lady Wisdom and the life lessons she is teaching us. I also suggest that you read 1 Corinthians 1:18–31 and 2:1–16. In these passages the Apostle Paul explains that Jesus Christ is the Wisdom of God.

Special Note

If you are performing before an audience of both men and women, you may add "sons of Adam" to the Storyteller's introduction. ("Hark! Listen! The Voice of Wisdom is calling you, daughters of God, sisters of Eve, sons of Adam!") In addition, the Storyteller's reference to "women" may be changed to "people."

The Characters

There are actually two characters in this dramatic monologue: Lady Wisdom and the Storyteller. Both may be portrayed by the same person, or the monologue can be presented as a two-person drama.

Lady Wisdom

Lady Wisdom is reciting the Voice of Wisdom from the Proverbs of Solomon. The Voice of Wisdom is not a physical person, even though she is called Lady Wisdom in the book of Proverbs; rather, she is the personification of wisdom. The Voice of Wisdom is a figure intended to represent an abstract truth. Solomon was inspired by God to teach His truths of wisdom through the voice of Lady Wisdom. Lady Wisdom tells us repeatedly throughout the Book of Proverbs that obeying, respecting, and fearing God brings wisdom, knowledge, understanding, and life. Lady Wisdom shows us that wisdom brings life, but the woman Folly brings death.

The Storyteller

The Storyteller reveals that the wisdom of God is His Son, Jesus Christ, who was with God before the creation of the world. The Apostle Paul clearly tells us this in 1 Corinthians 1:18–31 and 2:1–16. Jesus was with God before the beginning of time; Jesus was with God when He created the world; Jesus is the wisdom of God. Only by following the teachings of Jesus and walking in His footsteps can wisdom be attained.

The Character's Relevance to Our Lives Today

Most, if not all, of us want to be wise. Lady Wisdom reveals the path to wisdom in the book of Proverbs. Lady Wisdom's teachings will help us to become women of wisdom.

The Storyteller reveals Jesus Christ as the source of all wisdom. He was the wisdom with God before the beginning of time. By following Christ, our redeemer, and giving our lives to Him, we can obtain wisdom and become whole.

Stage Direction

Lady Wisdom embodies all the lessons taught in the book of Proverbs regarding wisdom. Feel free to move about the stage, use hand and arm gestures, and pause for dramatic effect as you portray this spiritual Voice of Wisdom. Lady Wisdom uses a different delivery of her speeches than is used by the other women in this book of monologues. With a strong voice, Lady Wisdom speaks more like a preacher or teacher. She is assertive, up front, and sure of herself. As you go through the memorization process and become familiar with the script and subject matter, you will sense the words or phrases that need to be emphasized. Think of yourself as a royal queen and speak slowly, confidently, and regally. This is a monologue that should not be rushed.

The Storyteller is a different character altogether and has a different delivery. A storyteller is folksy, exhibits friendliness and intimacy, and is dramatic in telling the story. This storyteller is a seer or prophet who is presenting Jesus as God's Wisdom and as the path and the way to eternal life.

Rehearse these two characters with the mindset that they are strong personalities who each bring the same message in her own way. Make a distinction in your mind between the two and make a difference in your delivery.

Biblical Setting

The setting for this drama is timeless. According to the book of Proverbs, Lady Wisdom was with God before creation. Wisdom is called a lady in the book of Proverbs, but in reality, we find in the New Testament that Jesus is the Wisdom of God. This is the final revelation at the end of the drama. Jesus was with God in the beginning, Jesus is with God now, Jesus will be with God forever—Jesus is God.

Stage Setting

The stage may be plain or decorated with flowers and/or potted plants.

Props

Lady Wisdom may choose to carry a basket of flowers, a Bible, or a scroll as she enters. If this is a one-woman portrayal, a coat tree, chair, or table may be used to hold the costume of the Storyteller. Lady Wisdom may leave her prop on this table as she places a cape or shawl over her costume and replaces her head covering with a hat. This costume change will denote the change of character. As the Storyteller, she may use a walking stick.

Costumes

Costumes for Two Women Performing

What would Lady Wisdom wear? You may be creative with Lady Wisdom's costume. However, I recommend a filmy, flowing robe or a Grecian-style gown, light in color. For a head covering she may wear a crown or a long head scarf of thin material. I wore a Grecian-type gown with a crown of dried flowers. Her feet may be bare, or she may wear sandals.

What would the Storyteller wear? I recommend a long skirt of any color, a colorful blouse, and shawl. A wide brimmed hat or scarf and simple sandals are also appropriate for this character.

Costumes for One Woman Performing

Lady Wisdom would wear the same costume as already described; however, she must make an on-stage transition from Lady Wisdom the Storyteller. A coat tree, table, or chair to the back or side of the stage holds the Storyteller costume of a cape (either short or long) and a hat or scarf. A walking stick is optional. Lady Wisdom will slip the cape on over her costume, remove her headpiece, and don the storyteller hat. This is done in full view of the audience. Don't rush—make this a part of the drama. The audience will be fascinated.

Refer to Production Ideas for more information.

Makeup

You can add makeup to enhance the appearance of Lady Wisdom. Foundation, eye shadow, eye liner, light rouge, and lipstick are suggested. However, apply makeup lightly if you are performing both Lady Wisdom and Storyteller, as the Storyteller is a character who would wear little makeup.

Length or Run Time of Monologue:

This monologue is fifteen to twenty minutes long, depending upon your presentation and whether or not a musical accompaniment is included at the beginning or end.

Mary of Nazareth—Mother of Jesus
Photo by Teres Ryan

CHAPTER 6

MARY OF NAZARETH— MOTHER OF JESUS

(Mary enters with a smile as she walks to center stage.)

Greetings! I am Mary of Nazareth, mother of Jesus. As you can see, I am an old woman now. My footsteps falter, and my skin is wrinkled with age.

(Mary sits on a bench or chair, up-stage center, as she describes the fig tree.)

In the heat of summer, I sit here in the shade beneath the leafy branches of the fig tree, alone with my memories. And in the chill of winter, I sit here in the sun beneath the barren branches of the fig tree, alone with my memories—memories filled with joy as well as sorrow.

Everyone seems to know who I am and where I live, for a day seldom passes that someone doesn't knock at my door asking to hear about my Son and about our lives. And I always invite them, as I invite you, to sit here with me beneath the fig tree as I gladly tell my story.

I was born and raised and have spent most of my life in this small village of Nazareth. As a young girl, shortly after I had reached my womanhood, I was betrothed to Joseph the carpenter. We had known since childhood that one day we would be married, but neither of us was prepared for God's intervention in our lives.

(Mary rises from the chair and walks to down-stage center.)

You see, to give birth to the long-awaited Messiah was the dream of every Hebrew girl of the tribe of Judah, and I was no exception. But God had not spoken to His people in over four hundred years. When the Angel Gabriel suddenly appeared to me, I was terrified and paralyzed by fear. I could not move! I could not breath! And when I gazed upon him, I was filled with wonderment and awe.

He spoke to me with a commanding voice; yet at the same time, his voice was kind and reassuring as he said, "Greetings, you who are highly favored! The Lord is with you."[1]

I was greatly troubled at his words, and I wondered what kind of greeting this might be.

But the angel continued, "Do not be afraid, Mary, you have found favor with God. You will be with child and give birth to a Son and you are to give Him the name Jesus. He will be great and will be called the Son of the Most High. The Lord God will give Him the throne of His father David, and He will reign over the house of Jacob forever; His kingdom will never end."[2]

When I heard these words, my head began to swirl, and my legs gave way beneath me. I fell to my knees and was barely able to whisper, "How will this be, since I am a virgin?"[3]

The angel explained, "The Holy Spirit will come upon you, and the power of the Most High will overshadow you. So, the Holy One to be born will be called the Son of God. Even Elizabeth your relative is going to have a child in her old age, and she who is said to be barren is in her sixth month. For nothing is impossible with God."[4]

As I knelt there on the ground, the words of the angel Gabriel washed over me like the waves of the sea. I was overwhelmed with feelings of confusion and doubt. Was this angel truly God's messenger? He said I had been chosen! From all the maidens in Judah, God had chosen me to be the mother of the long-awaited Messiah. Faith drove out my confusion and doubt and filled my heart with confidence and joy. I fell with my face to the ground in worship of God and cried, "I am the Lord's servant. May it be to me as you have said."[5]

When I raised my head, the angel was gone, and I was alone. When I thought of telling my parents and Joseph, I found that my confidence and joy had gone with the angel. Would they believe me? Would they think I had lost my mind? When they saw proof that I was with child, would my father beat me and turn me out of his house? Would Joseph despise me and desert me? Would the townspeople shun me, or worse yet, would the elders order me stoned to death in the street like a harlot? I was frightened and terrified.

Then I thought of what the angel had said regarding my kinswoman, Elizabeth. I would go to her; she would understand. And so I made the journey from Nazareth to the hill country of Judea where Elizabeth lived. As I approached her home, I called out a greeting.

When Elizabeth heard my voice, she cried, "Blessed are you among women, and blessed is the child you will bear! But why am I so favored that the mother of my Lord should come to me? As soon as the sound of your greeting reached my ears, the baby in my womb leaped for joy. Blessed is she who has believed that what the Lord has said to her will be accomplished."[6]

(Mary's Song)

When I heard Elizabeth's words, I praised the Most High: "My soul glorifies the Lord, and my spirit rejoices in God my

Savior, for He has been mindful of the humble state of His servant. From now on all generations will call me blessed, for the Mighty One has done great things for me—Holy is His name!"[7]

(Mary speaks with confidence.)

I stayed with Elizabeth for about three months before returning home. Elizabeth was a great help to me, and my heart was at peace. I had faith that God would take care of His Son and also of me, and I was no longer afraid.

In the meantime, God's messenger, the angel Gabriel, appeared to Joseph in a dream saying, "Joseph, son of David, do not be afraid to take Mary home as your wife, because what is conceived in her is from the Holy Spirit. She will give birth to a Son, and you are to give Him the name Jesus, because He will save His people from their sins."[8]

Upon awakening, Joseph remembered what the angel had said and also the words of the prophet Isaiah, "The virgin shall be with child and will give birth to a Son, and they will call Him Immanuel—which means God with us."[9]

When I returned to Nazareth from my visit with Elizabeth, Joseph took me home with him as his wife, but we had no union until after Jesus was born.

A short time before the birth of Jesus, Joseph and I had to make the seventy-mile trip from Nazareth to Bethlehem in order to register for the Roman census. I was great with child, and the journey was difficult. I had to either walk along the road, which was dusty, uneven, and sometimes steep, or be jostled up and down on the bony back of a donkey. We slept at night on the hard, rocky ground. My mother had begged me not to go. She feared that this strenuous journey would endanger the lives of both the baby and me. But I assured her that the Lord God would protect me and His Holy One.

When we at last arrived in Bethlehem, I was exhausted,

hungry, and cold. And the pains of childbirth were upon me. The city was teeming with multitudes of people who had also come to register. They were pushing and shoving, trying to find lodging for the night. We could find no place to stay, no place to rest. Looking back on that night, I know it was God's hand that led us away from the noisy crowds to the small hay-strewn stable filled with warmth created by the gentle cows and sheep.

And there on the hay I gave birth to the Son of God—the long-awaited Messiah, the Savior of the World. I was young and had never experienced childbirth, but the Lord Most High provided for me. I lovingly wrapped my baby in swaddling clothes and put Him to my breast. I remembered the words the angel had spoken to me, and I knew the prophecies of old. I was God's handmaiden, and He had chosen me to be the earthly mother of His Son. This was God's doing. I trusted Him to take care of us, for God is always faithful to His word.

I looked into my husband's eyes and whispered, "This child is bone of my bone and flesh of my flesh. I carried Him beneath my heart for nine months, and in that respect, He is mine and completely human. However, He is God's Son incarnate—not born of an earthly father but born of the Holy Spirit—and in that respect, He belongs to God and is completely divine. He is completely man and completely God. Can you comprehend that, Joseph?"

I gently placed the baby in His manger bed. Joseph and I fell to our knees, worshipping Him, our hearts filled with love and adoration.

Suddenly the stable was filled with excited shepherds, all talking at once and asking to see the newborn child—the Savior, Christ the Lord. They told us about the bright light from heaven; the glory of the Lord that shone around them on the hillside; the appearance of the angels; and the great company of heavenly hosts who were praising God and proclaiming "Glory to God in the highest and on earth peace to men on whom His favor rests."[10]

After the shepherds had seen the baby and worshipped Him, they rushed out to spread the news and repeat the words the angels had spoken. All who heard them were amazed, but I treasured the words of the angels and pondered them in my heart.

When the baby was eight days old, He was circumcised, and we named Him Jesus, the name the angel had given Him. According to the Law of Moses, we took Jesus to the temple in Jerusalem to consecrate Him to the Lord.

We met two elderly people in the temple that day, Simeon and Anna. They were prophets of God who were filled with the Holy Spirit. They both recognized Jesus as the Lord's Christ and prophesied regarding Him. Then Simeon blessed us and said to me, "This child is destined to cause the falling and rising of many in Israel, and to be a sign that will be spoken against, so that the thoughts of many hearts will be revealed. And a sword will pierce your own soul too."[11] These words frightened me, and I did not understand their meaning.

We returned to Bethlehem, and it came to pass that we were visited by a group of kings called magi or wise men. They were magnificently dressed in royal robes; they wore precious stones upon their fingers and gold chains around their necks. They said they had followed a star from a faraway country in the East, a star that was leading them to a newborn king. They entered the house and immediately bowed down and worshiped Jesus, calling Him the King of the Jews. Then they opened their treasures and presented Jesus with gifts of gold, frankincense, and myrrh. Joseph and I had never seen such riches!

When the Magi had gone, the angel of the Lord appeared to Joseph in a dream and said, "Get up and take the child and His mother and escape to Egypt. Stay there until I tell you, for Herod is going to search for the child and kill Him."[12]

Fear gripped our hearts as we packed up what little we had and set off for Egypt. God had generously provided for us through the gifts of the magi, for they gave us the means for our travel and our sojourn in Egypt. After Herod died, the angel of the Lord once more spoke to Joseph and told us to return to Israel, and we settled in Nazareth in Galilee.

Every year thereafter we made a trip to Jerusalem to celebrate the Feast of the Passover. When Jesus was twelve years old, we went up to the feast as was our custom. When the feast was over, we started home with a large group of people from Nazareth, not knowing that Jesus had stayed behind in Jerusalem. We traveled on for a whole day thinking He was with our group. At the end of the day, we began looking for Him among our relatives and friends, but He was nowhere to be found.

Joseph and I left the group and retraced our steps back to Jerusalem. With anxiety mounting in our hearts, we searched for three days for Jesus, praying to God to lead us to Him. At last we went into the temple courts and there we found Him, sitting among the teachers of the law, listening to them and asking them questions. Everyone who heard Jesus was amazed at His understanding.

Joseph and I were astonished, and I said to Jesus, "Son, why have you treated us like this? Your father and I have been anxiously searching for you."[13]

Jesus replied, "Why were you searching for me? Didn't you know I had to be in my Father's house?"[14]

(Mary speaks slowly.) As I looked at Jesus there in the temple that day, I sensed a change in Him. He was no longer my little boy. **(Mary takes a short pause.)** A cold chill ran through my body, and voices filled my head.

(Mary is distressed. She puts her hands on her head as she tries to escape the voices; turmoil and agony are seen in her face. There is pain in her voice as she repeats the voices that are echoing through her head.)

He is not your son … He is the Son of the Most High … He belongs to God … He will be called Emanuel … He will reign as king on the throne of David ... His kingdom will never end ... He will save His people from their sins ... and a sword will pierce your own soul too!

(Mary speaks to the audience.) How and when these things would come to pass was a mystery to me. I blindly took Jesus by the hand, and He obediently followed me as I stumbled out of the temple.

(Mary sighs deeply and walks across the stage. The mood changes here from distress and anxiety to smiles of happiness as she remembers the childhood of Jesus.)

Jesus brought us so much joy! He was a wonderful son— so caring, compassionate, kind, and loving to everyone. He obediently worked alongside Joseph in his carpenter shop and showed His love for me in so many ways. "He grew in wisdom and stature, and in favor with God and men."[15] As He grew older, Jesus spent more time in solitude, prayer, and communion with God, often going alone into the hills and staying for hours.

(Mary's mood now turns to nostalgia.)

When Jesus was thirty years old, He left our home to begin His public ministry, and my life changed forever. Many adored Him and followed Him, but many hated Him. His ministry lasted but three short years, and instead of a kingly crown as I had supposed, it ended with His death on a cross, suspended between two thieves. And my soul was indeed pierced with a sword.

(Mary gives this last speech with emotion and agony.)

Jesus, who was mine for one brief moment in time—from the cradle to the cross—now sits at the right hand of God on the throne of heaven. But He will always live in my heart just as He lives in your heart and in the heart of every believer.

Jesus came from heaven to earth to live as man and to die as God. He offered himself up as the sacrificial lamb—without spot or blemish—once and for all for the sins of the world, my sins and yours.

He will return to earth one day, not as a baby, but as Christ the King. He will come on the clouds of the sky with power and great glory, surrounded by the angels of heaven.

There is so much more I could tell you about Jesus, but the sun is setting, and you must be on your way. Please come again and sit with me here beneath the fig tree, for talking about Jesus is such a blessing.

(Mary smiles and bows her head as she gives her parting words.)

And now I bid you, shalom. Go in God's peace.

End of drama.

PRODUCTION NOTES AND RECOMMENDATIONS

Scriptures

Matthew, chapters 1 and 2; Luke, chapters 1 and 2.

The Character

The Virgin Mary is without doubt the most famous woman of the New Testament. She was chosen by God when she was yet a young teen to bear His Son, Jesus, and rear Him in a devout Hebrew home. Books, songs, and prayers have been written in honor of Mary. Even though she was chosen by God and blessed among women, Mary speaks very little in the Bible other than in the gospel of Luke (chapters 1 and 2) and in the gospel of John (chapter 2). Upon several occasions, Mary is referred to. She is placed near the cross of Jesus (John chapter 19) and in the upper room where the disciples waited for the Holy Spirit to descend (Acts chapter 1).

The Character's Relevance to Our Lives

When Mary first heard the angel's decree—that she had found favor with God and that she would be with child and give birth to the Son of God—she was shocked, and asked the angel, "How will this be since I am a virgin?"

When the angel explained what was to happen, Mary responded, "I am the Lord's servant. May it be to me as you have said."

We learn faith, trust, and acceptance from Mary. She didn't refuse; she didn't say let me think about this before I give you an answer; she didn't ask how this would affect Joseph, her betrothed husband; and she did not ask how her parents and the community would receive this news. She accepted the shocking news in faith and with trust in God.

Our Triune God still asks for faith, trust, and acceptance from us. He still expects total obedience from us without counting the cost. When God says "Go!" we won't ask why, or how far, or is it safe. When God says "Love your neighbor as yourself," we won't ask which one and for how long. When God says "Follow Me," we won't procrastinate or refuse. Like Mary, we will grasp God's hand and travel the road with Him over the smooth paths and over the rocks and pitfalls as we journey onward to our heavenly home.

Stage Directions

If you are a young woman, you can omit the second two sentences in which Mary describes herself as old. You can start with, "Greetings! I am Mary of Nazareth, mother of Jesus. In the heat of summer, I sit here in the shade ..." Whatever your age, the decision is yours to make.

Feel free to move about the stage as you go from one emotion or one subject to another. Even a small movement of your head or body will help change the mood. Avoid eye contact with the audience, which can cause you to lose your place in the drama and your characterization. Looking directly over the audience just above their heads to the back of the room will give the illusion that you are looking at them.

Biblical Setting

The setting is Mary's home in the village of Nazareth, sometime after Jesus's death and ascension. It is possible that Mary is a widow and that she lives alone.

Stage Setting

This drama does not require a stage setting other than a bench, stool, or chair for Mary to sit upon as she describes the fig tree. However, if you desire, you can decorate the stage with flowers, potted plants, or clay pots, baskets, or candles.

Properties (Props)

Mary may use a walking stick upon entering to emphasis her age. She can lay it on the floor beneath or beside her chair when she sits. This prop is optional.

Costume

Mary would wear a long dress in the biblical style with a head scarf and sandals. She could wear a cloak if you so desire. Details on costumes can be found in Production Ideas.

Length or Run Time of Monologue

This monologue is twenty-five to thirty minutes long depending on your portrayal.

Mary Magdalene—in the Garden
(photo by Teres Ryan)

CHAPTER 7

MARY MAGDALENE—
IN THE GARDEN

(Mary Magdalene enters the stage carrying a basket containing herbs and spices that she will use to anoint the body of Jesus. Mary walks to center stage where she looks out at the audience and begins to speak in an intensely excited voice.)

We women came to the garden at sunrise on the first day of the week bearing herbs and spices to anoint the body of our Lord. It was dawn when we entered the garden, and the dew still clung to the grass, the leaves, and the flowers. We were stunned to see that the huge rock had been rolled away from the entrance of the tomb, and when we looked inside **(Mary gasps in amazement.)**, the body was gone! The body of our Lord was not there!

Ah, forgive me. My thoughts run ahead of my story. Let me start at the beginning.

(Mary turns and takes a few steps toward the back or side of the stage and sets the basket down. She then walks down stage and speaks to audience in a friendly voice.)

I am Mary of Magdala, also called Mary Magdalene. I am thus called because I was born and raised in the town of Magdala, which is situated on the shores of the Sea of Galilee near Capernaum. You have undoubtedly heard of me, but there is much confusion as to my true identity. I have been confused with Mary of Bethany. I have also been confused with the sinful woman who dried the Master's feet with her hair. And I have been mistaken for the adulterous woman brought to Jesus by the Pharisees. But I am none of those women. There are also those who say that I was a harlot, but this is not true. You can search the Holy Scriptures, and you will never find it mentioned that Mary Magdalene was a harlot.

As a young Hebrew girl child, I was taught the scriptures at home, and I learned that one day a Messiah would appear and reign on the throne of David. When I became a woman, I tried to faithfully obey the Law of Moses. But there was one dreadful blight upon my life.

(At this point Mary becomes gradually agitated, building to a crescendo at the end of her speech.)

I suffered from a terrible disease—a horrible sickness. At times I would be possessed by demons. When they would ravage me, I would suddenly fall to the ground, writhing in a blind stupor. I would thrash my arms and legs in the air and screech, howl, and babble. Foam would come from my mouth, I would gnash my teeth, and even swallow my tongue if it were not prevented.

(In the following speech, Mary is subdued and hopelessly defeated as she describes her past life.)

When the demons were done with me, I would lie upon the ground as if dead. For many days thereafter, I would lie upon my bed, too sick and weak to move. I had no future, and I was, of all women, most desolate. What decent Hebrew man would take me for a wife? I was shunned, avoided, and alone. My life was bleak and hopeless, and as time went by, I became more and more bitter and cynical.

(Hopefulness is now reflected in her voice and in the smile on her face as Mary describes meeting Jesus.)

Then came the day that I met Jesus, and He changed my life forever! As long as I live, I will never forget that day. I had followed the crowds of people out into the country where, there on a hillside, Jesus sat beneath the shade of a tree. He was teaching the people and healing them. Yes, healing them of all manner of sickness and disease. My greatest desire was to be healed. I tried to make my way to Him through the throng of people, but it was no use.

As I desperately pushed and shoved, suddenly a great calm came over me. **(She closes her eyes and smiles, folding her hands over her breast as she speaks the word *calm*.)** I felt His arms reach out and encircle me in a warm embrace. I was a child again, safe and secure in the arms of love. **(She opens her eyes now and looks out over the audience, speaking in awe.)** And then—I cannot tell you how it happened—I found myself standing before Him looking into His face. I was held spellbound by His eyes. They were clear and deep, and as I gazed into them, I was bathed in a warm, dazzling light. A feeling of endless peace and love enveloped me.

(Mary reflects this calmness and peace in her movements, face, and voice. She seems mesmerized as she describes His voice.)

And then He spoke, and His voice was beautiful. It was the music of a golden harp playing, the chiming of silver bells, the sighing of the wind through the olive trees, the rushing of many waters. **(At this point Mary's voice is strong and rises to a crescendo.)** And when He spoke to the demons within me, His voice was the sound of mighty, rolling thunder, and His words drove those demons from my body never to return.[1] I was healed! I was whole! I was alive for the first time in my life. As I looked into His face, I knew that I looked not into the face of man, but into the face of God, and I fell to the ground, worshiping Him.

(Mary takes a few steps to one side, signifying a change in her story as she tells about her life after Jesus healed her.)

After Jesus healed me, I was a new woman. His grace and love had replaced all my bleakness and bitterness. My only purpose in life now was to follow Him and serve Him all the rest of my days. I did return to Magdala, however, just long enough to settle my affairs, for I was a woman of much substance. I sold all that I had and laid the money at my Master's feet. There were other women who had been healed by Jesus who did the same thing—Johanna and Suzanna among them.[2]

We women became the first female disciples of our Lord. We looked after the needs of Jesus and the twelve, using our money to purchase food and needed supplies in nearby villages. We made camp in the evenings, setting up the goat skin tents and laying out the mats for sleeping. We cooked and served the food and washed the clothing. And on many occasions, after supper, I would lovingly wash the tired and dusty feet of my Master, laying out a fresh robe for the morrow.

Now, none of the chosen twelve were women, but that was of no concern to us, for Jesus honored women. He made us feel worthy, valued, equal. He taught that God loves all His children in the same way and that God is no respecter of one person above another. And in God's kingdom there is no male or female! Jesus did not look upon women or children as did the world. He did not look upon us as mere chattel, possessions, slaves, oh no. Jesus elevated us to heights the world had never known.

For of children He said, "Let the little children come to me, and do not hinder them, for the kingdom of heaven belongs to such as these."[3]

And as for women—to whom did our Lord first reveal himself after His resurrection? And who was the one who proclaimed the greatest news the world has ever heard: "He is risen." It was I, a woman. Scripture teaches that this was no accident. This was in God's plan. What greater honor could our lord heap upon the head of woman?[4]

(Mary walks across the stage on the next sentence and back to center stage on the second sentence.)

Day after day, month after month, we traversed the hills and valleys, towns, and villages of Galilee and Judea. I watched Jesus as He moved among the people, as He taught them, as He healed them, as He loved them. And I began to slowly understand more and more of His message and His purpose. We women understood our Lord more readily than did the twelve. As women and mothers, we understood the great love He had for the people. We understood His gentleness, His compassion. Some say God has gifted women in a special way. Some call it a sixth sense.

There were those followers who had a problem with the gentleness of Jesus, especially Judas Iscariot and his friends the Zealots. They looked at Christ's meekness as weakness. They did not understand His mission. They were anxiously waiting for Him to ride forth into Jerusalem as a mighty warrior leading the armies of Israel behind Him. They expected Him to overthrow the harsh Roman rule and set Himself up as king on the throne of David.

There were also those unbelievers who scoffed and jeered at Jesus, and you no doubt know about the Pharisees and Sadducees who continually tried to trick and trap Jesus regarding the Law of Moses. Then there were the spies of King Herod and the informants of the Sanhedrin. And always in the shadows, the Roman soldiers lurked, watching His every move. As time went by, I feared greatly for the safety of my Master. And then came the fateful day when Jesus announced that we would go up to Jerusalem to keep the Passover.

Oh, we were happy and joyful as we traveled along. As we neared Jerusalem, the cheering crowds of people lined the roadway shouting, "Hosanna! Blessed is He who comes in the name of the Lord." Some spread their cloaks on the road before Him, and still others cut branches from the palm trees and laid them on His path shouting, "Blessed is the coming kingdom of our father David! Hosanna in the highest."[5]

(Mary's next speech builds in intensity and power as she uses her voice and body to build to a final crescendo, which ends in the words "death and destruction.")

But little did we know what was in store for our Lord. For Jerusalem was a seething cauldron of turmoil centered around this man Jesus. There was the urgency of the Zealots to announce Him king; the jealousy and hatred of the chief priests and the Pharisees; the suspicions and fears of King Herod; the might and power of Pontius Pilate and the Roman Empire; and the fickle-minded, easily swayed multitudes of people.

All these forces came together in Jerusalem like the mighty whirlwind of the desert which draws and sucks everything in its path *up, up, up* into its swirling, twirling funnel of death and destruction! **(She takes a short pause.)**

(Mary delivers this next speech with quiet desperation.)

Into this our gentle Savior rode on the back of a small donkey as a sheep to the slaughter.

We women were there through it all. We were there in the Upper Room as the Passover meal was prepared; we followed in the shadows as He went to the Mount of Olives to pray; we huddled in the darkness as He was arrested; we followed the throng as He was brought before the Sanhedrin for trial and after that to Pilate, then on to Herod, and finally back to Pilate. We were there as He was beaten and sentenced to death.

(She delivers this next speech with compassion, fear, and dismay.)

We saw Him spat upon and mocked, flogged, and scourged. Have you seen the Roman whip used for flogging? It is no ordinary whip—it is an instrument of death! The whip is made of many leather thongs, and attached to the end of each thong is a piece of sharp bone or lead. With this whip they beat our Master until ribbons of bloody flesh hung from His back. He endured a beating which no man could ever survive.

They slapped Him and hit Him in the face with their fists. They beat Him over the head with a heavy staff, and when He could no longer stand alone, they put a purple robe upon Him and forced a crown of thorns upon His brow. The thorns, as sharp as razors, pierced His flesh causing the blood to flow down His face onto the robe. Then they bowed down before Him in a mockery of worship.

(Mary delivers this speech with tears of fear and hopelessness in her voice.)

After Jesus was sentenced to die, they removed the robe and thrust a heavy wooden cross upon His bloody back. We followed as the soldiers forced Him to carry the cross through the streets of Jerusalem up to the hill of Golgotha. But He was so weakened from that night of beating and torture that He moved slowly, staggering and falling under the weight of that cross. The impatient soldiers beat and kicked Him until He had no strength to rise. Then they forced a bystander, Simon of Cyrene, to help Him carry the cross up onto the hill of crucifixion.

We women never left Him. The men did, save John. John alone remained at the cross with us. We clung to each other in horror. We held His mother Mary up lest she fall into a swoon. Think of her grief. Put yourself in her place. Imagine seeing your beloved son—your child who nursed at your breast—beaten, mocked, spat upon, and, as you stand helplessly by, murdered in the most horrible manner imaginable: *crucifixion.*

(Mary places her hands over her ears, closes her eyes, and bows her head in agony.)

Oh, the sounds of the hammer are still resounding in my ears, and I can see the nails tearing flesh. Oh, I cannot bear too speak of it further. **(Mary lowers her hands and raises her head to the audience.)** And neither could God the Father bear to look upon it, for at midday the sky was darkened. At the moment of our Lord's death, the earth did shake, the curtain of the temple was torn in two from top to bottom, rocks split open, and the dead came forth from the tombs and prophesied throughout the city.

(Now for a scene change. Mary walks to the side, then turns back to the audience, emotions under control.)

Joseph of Arimathea, who was a believer and a wealthy man, asked Pilate for permission to bury Jesus. Nicodemus helped Joseph take that precious body from the cross. We women followed as they took our Lord's body to be buried in Joseph's own tomb. This tomb, in which never a body had lain, was in a beautiful garden situated on the sunny slopes of the upper city. Joseph's gardener tended well the olive trees, the grape arbor, and the many flowers and shrubs. It was indeed a lovely place to lay the body of our Lord.

We women watched as Joseph and Nicodemus gently laid our Lord's body in the tomb. They wrapped the long grave cloths around and around His body, along with the spices that Nicodemus had brought. Then they placed the burial cloth around His head.

Since the Sabbath was upon us, there was no time to finish the Jewish ritual of burial; therefore, we women planned to return on the first day of the week, bringing more herbs and spices to complete the burial. As the two men pushed the heavy stone over the door of the tomb, we left the garden with hearts as heavy as that stone.

Oh, I thought that Sabbath would never end! Early in the morning on the first day of the week, we women went to the garden, bearing our baskets of herbs and spices. We were in such grief that we did not notice the beauty of the dew-drenched garden. We were preoccupied with how we would manage to move the stone from the mouth of the tomb. As we approached the tomb, we saw, through the shadows, that the stone had already been rolled away. How could that be? We moved forward and looked inside—He was not there! The body of our lord was gone!

We dropped our baskets and ran from the garden through the streets to the house where the others were staying. I pounded on the door shouting, "They have taken the Lord out of the tomb, and we don't know where they have put Him!"[6]

They did not believe us at first, but then Peter and John rose up and ran to the tomb. We followed, and when we arrived, they were inside the tomb, and they saw that we spoke the truth. There the grave cloths lay, just as they had been wound around our Lord's body, and the head cloth was folded to the side by itself. None of us knew what to think. Jesus was dead! His body had disappeared! All hope was lost. He had tried all along to tell us what would happen, but we had not fully understood.

Everyone finally left the garden, filled with despair. But I could not leave; something held me to that spot. With tears flowing down my face, I looked once more into the tomb, and there I saw two angels, all in white, seated where our Lord's body had lain. One was seated where our Lord's head had rested; the other, where His feet had lain. They asked me why I was crying, and I replied, "They have taken my Lord away and I don't know where they have put Him."[7]

And in fear and trembling, I turned and saw a man behind me. At first glance, I thought He was the gardener, and He said to me, "Woman, why are you crying? Who is it you are looking for?"[8]

I replied, "Sir, if you have carried Him away, tell me where you have put Him, and I will get Him."[9]

I turned to look for His body among the bushes, and then the man spoke my name, "Mary."[10]

At that moment I recognized the voice of my Master! My eyes were opened, and I cried out, *"Rabboni!"* and fell to the ground to kiss His feet.[11]

But Jesus stopped me by saying, "Do not hold on to me, for I have not yet returned to the Father. Go instead to my brothers and tell them that I am returning to my Father and your Father, to my God and your God."[12]

At this command, I ran like the wind through the streets and burst into the house shouting, "He lives! I have seen the Lord! He lives!"[13]

(Mary delivers the next speech with exuberance and joy. This is the story's application.)

Oh, yes, my sisters and brothers. I, Mary Magdalene, stand before you today to testify to the fact that Jesus the Nazarene, the carpenter of Galilee, is the Son of God, the Savior of the world. He drove seven demons from my body. I was with Him in His ministry. I was there at His trial. I saw Him crucified. I saw Him buried. And I saw Him alive after His resurrection. I have been greatly blessed, but you, my friends, will receive the greater blessings. For I saw and believed, but you have not seen, yet you have believed. How greatly you are blessed by God the Father.

(Transition. Mary turns and picks up the basket.)

I do not come often to Jerusalem, but this garden is always with me in my heart. I come to it each morning, and here I meet my risen Savior. "He walks with me, and He talks with me, and He tells me I am His own."

I invite you, too, to visit this garden each morning. Meet Jesus here. Open your heart to Him. Give Him your cares, your trials, your pain, your sorrow, your brokenness, your sin. And He will give to you His blessings, His love, His peace, His joy, His mercy, and His pardon. He will hold you, too, in His arms of love, and you, too, will be made whole.

And now, as I depart, I pray that you will allow the peace that passes all understanding to dwell in your hearts until that day when Jesus comes again to call us all unto Himself. Until that day, I bid you shalom. **(Mary bows.)**

End of drama.

PRODUCTION NOTES AND RECOMMENDATIONS

Scriptures

Jesus healed Mary from seven demons; she became a follower of Jesus and donated money to His ministry:

Luke 8:1–3

Mary was at the cross when Jesus died:

Matthew 27:45–56; Mark 15;33–41; Luke 23:44-49; John 19:25–27

Mary was there when Jesus was buried:

Matthew 27:57–61; Mark 15:42–47; Luke 23:50–56;

Mary was first to see that Jesus had risen from the dead:

Matthew 28:1–7; Mark 16: 1–8; Luke 24:1–10; John 20:1–2

Jesus appeared to Mary after His resurrection:

Matthew 28:8–10: Mark 16:9–11; John 20:10–18

The Character

Mary Magdalene was from the seaport town of Magdala, which is a town in Israel. She is mentioned sixteen times by name in the New Testament. In ten of these passages, her name heads the list, implying that she occupied a place of prominence among godly women. She is first mentioned in Luke 8:1–3 as the woman from whom Jesus cast seven demons. There is no indication that she was a prostitute as has often been attributed to her. She has been confused with the prostitute in Luke 7:37–38 who washed Jesus's feet with her tears, dried them with her hair, and then anointed them with perfume.

After Jesus healed her, Mary Magdalene became His faithful disciple and followed Him as He ministered. She was at the foot of the cross when Jesus was crucified, she was there when He was buried, and she was the first to see Him after He arose from the dead. I am certain that she was with the gathering of believers who watched as He ascended into heaven fifty days later.

The Character's Relevance to Our Lives

Mary Magdalene was a faithful follower of Jesus. She left her comfortable home and family to follow Jesus, and she gave her own money to support His ministry. The fact that God chose Mary Magdalene as the first person to see the risen Savior lends great credibility to Mary and to Christian women in general. Mary is an example of a woman who gave everything she had to her Lord. I believe this is the greatest drama because it is the story of Jesus' ministry, trial, death, and resurrection. This drama touches hearts to come to Jesus in a meaningful way.

Stage Directions

Mary enters to center stage carrying a basket. At a certain time in the drama she sets the basket on the floor or on any convenient place—bench, chair, or table. Mary is free to move about the stage as she tells her story. Any change of movement can change the mood and tempo of the drama. At the end of the drama, Mary picks the basket up and carries it as she exits.

The Song

The Christian hymn, "In the Garden," was written by C. Austin Miles in 1913. He wrote the song after he had completed an inspiring study of the resurrection story (see John 20:10–18). He composed the song with Mary Magdalene in mind, since she was the first to recognize her Lord in the garden. This moving song is considered one of the favorite Christian hymns of all time throughout the world. This song is highly effective when sung with the drama. The first two stanzas can be sung at the beginning of the drama and the third stanza can be sung at the end.

Biblical Setting

The Biblical setting for this drama is Galilee, Judea, Jerusalem, and the garden in Jerusalem where Jesus was buried.

Stage Setting

The stage can be plain or decorated as a garden. Members of one church where I performed made large rocks of papier-mâché. At another church, members made large, three-dimensional rocks out of cardboard. In both churches, the "rocks" were surrounded by potted shrubs and baskets of flowers to designate a garden. The decoration would be at the discretion of the host group. Most of the time, I performed this drama on a bare stage. The stage setting is not your responsibility; however, I include ideas that your church might want to use.

Properties (Props)

Mary enters the stage carrying a basket filled with artificial green plants representing herbs to be used for Jesus's burial. This basket can be a shallow basket that is carried in your hands, or it can be a basket with a handle. A little greenery can be peaking over the sides of the basket.

Costume

Mary wears a plain robe in a muted blue or brown color, a covering for her head, and sandals.

Makeup

Women in Israel at that time, did not wear makeup. However, in a large room and under stage lighting Mary Magdalene's facial features may need to be accentuated. Start with a neutral facial foundation and add mascara and eyeliner to delineate the eyes. A light and natural lip gloss and cheek blush can be added.

Length or Run Time

This monologue is thirty to thirty-five minutes in length. The song "In the Garden" will add five minutes more.

CHAPTER 8

MARY MAGDALENE—
HE IS RISEN

This drama is a shorter version of Mary Magdalene—In the Garden.

(Mary enters to center stage with a smile on her face.)

Greetings. I am Mary Magdalene. I am the woman whom Jesus healed by driving seven demons from my body. I knew then that He was the Messiah, and I became one of His most faithful followers. I, along with other women whom He healed, joined Him and His twelve disciples as they traveled throughout Judea on His mission of teaching and healing.

I'm standing in the garden where Jesus was buried. I saw Him placed in the tomb, and I saw Him three days later standing in this very garden. I was also in Jerusalem when He was crucified. Oh, I remember it as if it were yesterday. But let me start at the beginning of my story.

(Mary looks into the distance as she remembers the following incident.)

I remember the fateful day when Jesus announced that we

would go up to Jerusalem to keep the Passover. Oh, we were happy and joyful as we traveled along. As we neared Jerusalem, the cheering crowds of people lined the roadway shouting, "Hosanna, blessed is He who comes in the name of the Lord." Some spread their cloaks on the road before Him, and still others cut branches from the palm trees and laid them on His path shouting, "Blessed is the coming kingdom of our Father David! Hosanna in the highest"[1]

(Mary's next speech will build in intensity and power as she uses her voice and body to build to a final crescendo, which ends in the words "death and destruction.")

But little did we know what was in store for our Lord. For Jerusalem was a seething cauldron of turmoil centered around this man Jesus. There was the urgency of the Zealots to announce Him king; the jealousy and hatred of the chief priests and the Pharisees; the suspicions and fears of King Herod; the might and power of Pontius Pilate and the Roman Empire; and the fickle-minded, easily swayed multitudes of people. All these forces came together in Jerusalem like the mighty whirlwind of the desert which draws and sucks everything in its path *up, up, up* into its swirling, twirling, funnel of death and destruction!

(Mary delivers this next speech with quiet desperation.)

Into this our gentle Savior rode, as a sheep to the slaughter, on the back of a small donkey.

We women were there through it all. We were there in the Upper Room as the Passover meal was prepared; we followed in the shadows as He went to the Mount of Olives to pray; we huddled in the darkness as He was arrested; we followed the throng as He was brought before the Sanhedrin for trial. He was then taken to Pilate, then on to Herod, and finally back to Pilate. We were there as He was beaten and sentenced to death.

(She delivers this next speech with compassion, fear, and dismay.)

We saw Him spat upon and mocked, flogged, and scourged. Have you seen the Roman whip used for flogging? It is no ordinary whip—it is an instrument of death! The whip is made of many leather thongs, and attached to the end of each thong is a piece of sharp bone or lead. With this whip they beat our Master until ribbons of bloody flesh hung from His back.

He endured a beating which no man could ever survive. They slapped Him and hit Him in the face with their fists. They beat Him over the head with a heavy staff, and when He could no longer stand alone, they put a purple robe upon Him and forced a crown of thorns upon His brow. The thorns, as sharp as razors, pierced His flesh causing the blood to flow down His face onto the robe. Then they bowed down before Him in a mockery of worship.

(Mary delivers this speech with fear and hopelessness on her face and in her voice.)

After Jesus was sentenced to die, they removed the robe and thrust a heavy wooden cross upon His bloody back. We followed as the soldiers forced Him to carry the cross through the streets of Jerusalem up to the hill of Golgotha. But He was so weakened from that night of beating and torture that He moved slowly, staggering and falling under the weight of the cross. The impatient soldiers beat and kicked Him until He had no strength to rise. Then they forced a bystander, Simon of Cyrene, to help Him carry the cross up onto the hill of crucifixion.

We women never left Him. The men did, save John. John

alone remained at the cross with us. We clung to each other in horror. We held His mother Mary up lest she fall into a swoon. Think of her grief. Put yourself in her place. Imagine seeing your beloved son—your child who nursed at your breast—beaten, mocked, spat upon, and, as you stand helplessly by, murdered in the most horrendous manner imaginable—*crucifixion*.

(Mary places her hands over her ears, closes her eyes, and bows her head in agony.)

Oh, the sounds of the hammer are still resounding in my ears, and I can see the nails tearing the flesh. Oh, I cannot bear too speak of it further. (**Mary lowers her hands and raises her head to the audience.**) And neither could God the Father bear to look upon it, for at midday the sky was darkened. At the moment of our Lord's death, the earth did shake. The curtain of the temple was torn in two from top to bottom, rocks split open, and the dead came forth from the tombs and prophesied throughout the city.

(Now for a scene change. Mary walks to the side, then turns back to the audience, emotions under control.)

Joseph of Arimathea, who was a believer and a wealthy man, asked Pilate for permission to bury Jesus. Nicodemus helped Joseph take that precious body from the cross. We women followed as they took our Lord's body to be buried in Joseph's own tomb. This tomb, in which never a body had lain, was in a beautiful garden situated on the sunny slopes of the upper city. Joseph's gardener tended well the olive trees, the grape arbor, and the many flowers and shrubs. It was indeed a lovely place to lay the body of our Lord.

We women watched as Joseph and Nicodemus gently laid our Lord in the tomb. They wrapped the long grave cloths around and around His body, along with the spices that Nicodemus had brought. Then they placed the burial cloth around His head.

Since the Sabbath was upon us, there was no time to finish the Jewish ritual of burial; therefore, we women planned to return on the first day of the week, bringing more herbs and spices to complete the burial. As the two men pushed the heavy stone over the door of the tomb, we left the garden with hearts as heavy as that stone.

Oh, I thought that Sabbath would never end! Early in the morning on the first day of the week, we women went to the garden, bearing our baskets of herbs and spices. We were in such grief that we did not notice the beauty of the dew-drenched garden. We were preoccupied with how we would manage to move the stone from the mouth of the tomb. As we approached the tomb, we saw, through the shadows, that the stone had already been rolled away. How could that be? We moved forward and looked inside—He was not there! The body of our lord was gone!

We dropped our baskets and ran from the garden through the streets to the house where the others were staying. I pounded on the door shouting, "They have taken the Lord out of the tomb and we don't know where they have put Him!"[2]

They did not believe us at first, but then Peter and John rose up and ran to the tomb. We followed, and when we arrived, they were inside the tomb, and they saw that we spoke the truth. There the grave cloths lay, just as they had been wound around our Lord's body, and the head cloth was folded to the side by itself. None of us knew what to think. Jesus was dead! His body had disappeared! All hope was lost. He had tried all along to tell us what would happen, but we had not fully understood.

Everyone finally left the garden, filled with despair. But I could not leave; something held me to that spot. With tears flowing down my face, I looked once more into the tomb, and there I saw two angels, all in white. One was seated where our Lord's head had rested; the other, where His feet had lain. They asked me why I was crying, and I replied, "They have taken my Lord away and I don't know where they have put Him."[3]

In fear and trembling I turned and saw a man standing behind me. At first glance, I thought He was the gardener, and He said to me, "Woman, why are you crying? Who is it you are looking for?"[4]

I replied, "Sir, if you have carried Him away, tell me where you have put Him, and I will get Him."[5]

I turned to look for His body among the bushes, and then the man spoke my name, "Mary."[6]

At that moment I recognized the voice of my Master! My eyes were opened. I cried out, *"Rabboni!"*[7] and fell to the ground to kiss His feet.

But Jesus stopped me by saying, "Do not hold on to me, for I have not yet returned to the Father. Go instead to my brothers and tell them that I am returning to my Father and your Father, to my God and your God."[8]

At this command, I ran like the wind through the streets and burst into the house shouting, "He lives! I have seen the Lord! He lives!"[9]

(Mary delivers the next speech with exuberance and joy. It is the application of Mary's story.)

Oh, yes, my sisters and brothers. I, Mary Magdalene, stand before you today to testify to the fact that Jesus the Nazarene, the carpenter of Galilee, is the Son of God, the Savior of the world. He drove seven demons from my body. I was with Him in His ministry. I was there at His trial. I saw Him crucified. I saw Him buried. And I saw Him alive after His resurrection. I have been greatly blessed, but you, my friends, will receive the greater blessings. For I saw and believed, but you have not seen, yet you have believed. How greatly you are blessed by God the Father.

I do not come often to Jerusalem, but this garden is always

with me in my heart. I come to it each morning, and here I meet my risen Savior. "He walks with me, and He talks with me, and He tells me I am His own."

I invite you, too, to visit this garden each morning. Meet Jesus here. Open your heart to Him. Give Him your cares, your trials, your pain, your sorrow, your brokenness, your sin. And He will give to you His blessings, His love, His peace, His joy, His mercy, and His pardon. He will hold you, too, in His arms of love, and you, too, will be made whole.

And now, as I depart, I pray that you will allow the peace that passes all understanding to dwell in your hearts until that day when Jesus comes again to call us all unto Himself. Until that day, I bid you, shalom. **(Mary bows.)**

End of drama.

Production Notes and Recommendations

Scriptures

Jesus healed Mary from seven demons, she became a follower of Jesus, and donated money to His ministry:

Luke 8:1–3

Mary was at the cross when Jesus died:

Matthew 27:45-56; Mark 15;33–41; Luke 23:44–49; John 19:25–27

Mary was there when Jesus was buried:

Matthew 27:57–61; Mark 15:42–47; Luke 23:50–56;

Mary was first to see that Jesus had risen from the dead:

Matthew 28:1–7; Mark 16: 1–8; Luke 24:1–10; John 20:1–2

Jesus appeared to Mary after His resurrection:

Matthew 28:8–10: Mark 16:9–11; John 20:10–18

This is a short version of "Mary Magdalene—In the Garden." This version begins as Jesus enters Jerusalem on Palm Sunday and is therefore only half as long. This shorter version may by a better fit for an Easter Sunday worship service.

The Character

Mary Magdalene was from the seaport town of Magdala, which is a town in Israel. She is mentioned sixteen times by name in the New Testament. In ten of these passages her name heads the list, implying that she occupied a place of prominence among godly women. She is first mentioned in Luke 8:1–3 as the woman from whom Jesus cast seven demons. There is no indication that she was a prostitute as has often been attributed to her. She has been confused with the prostitute in Luke 7:37–38 who washed Jesus's feet with her tears, dried them with her hair, and then anointed them with perfume.

After Jesus healed her, Mary Magdalene became His faithful disciple and followed Him as He ministered. She was at the foot of the cross when Jesus was crucified, she was there when He was buried, and she was the first to see Him after He arose from the dead. I am certain that she was with the gathering of believers who watched as He ascended into heaven fifty days later.

The Character's Relevance to Our Lives

Mary Magdalene was a faithful follower of Jesus. She left her comfortable home and family to follow Jesus and gave her own money to support His ministry. The fact that God chose Mary Magdalene as the first person to see the risen Savior lends great credibility to Mary and to Christian women in general. Mary is an example of a woman who gave everything she had to her Lord. I believe this is the greatest drama because it is the story of Jesus' ministry, trial, death, and resurrection. This drama touches hearts to come to Jesus in a meaningful way.

Stage Directions

Mary enters to center stage. Mary is free to move about the stage as she tells her story. Any change of movement (head, arms, hands, turns) can change the mood and tempo of the drama.

The Song

The Christian hymn, "In the Garden," was written by C. Austin Miles in 1913. He wrote the song after he had completed an inspiring study of the resurrection story (see John 20:10–18). He composed the song with Mary Magdalene in mind, since she was the first to recognize her Lord in the garden. This moving song is considered one of the favorite Christian hymns worldwide. If you use this song with the drama, it is highly effective for a soloist or the audience to sing the first two stanzas at the beginning of the drama and the third stanza at the end.

Biblical Setting

Jerusalem is the Biblical setting for this drama.

Stage Setting

You may choose to have an empty stage, or if this is part of an Easter worship service, the stage may be quite full, and you will occupy on small section. Or you may want to go with the garden motif of shrubs and flowers to designate a garden.

Props

Mary has no props in this drama.

Costume

Mary wears a plain robe in a muted blue or brown color, a covering for her head, and sandals.

Makeup

Women in Israel at that time, did not wear makeup. However, in a large room and under stage lighting Mary Magdalene's facial features may need to be accentuated. Start with a neutral facial foundation and add mascara and eyeliner to delineate the eyes. A light and natural lip gloss and cheek blush can be added.

Length or Run Time of Monologue:

This monologue is fifteen to twenty minutes in length. The song "In the Garden" will add five minutes more to the length of the monologue.

CHAPTER 9

THE EASTER MIRACLE— AS SEEN THROUGH THE EYES OF MARY MAGDALENE

(Hymn: "Were You There" or song of your choice.)

(Mary Magdalene enters at the end of the song, or If she is already on stage, she stands and speaks at the end of the song.)

On many occasions, I walked by the hill of Golgotha, but I could never bear to look at those cruel crosses. However, today was different. Today I did not hurry by or look the other way. Today I climbed up that hill of execution. I was following a sorrowful procession of grim-faced men and weeping women. Leading the procession was the man Jesus. He was an innocent man who had been whipped, beaten, spat upon, mocked, scourged, flogged, and sentenced to die by crucifixion.

I was there. I saw it all. I know not how He endured that night of torture or how He had the strength to climb that hill. Of what was He guilty? What had He done? He had taught us to love others. He had taught us compassion. He had given us hope.

He had healed our bodies and our hearts. He was the son of God, and He was our Messiah. For this He was crucified. I fell at the foot of the cross where He hung, suspended between earth and heaven, and I wept as His life's blood ebbed away.

(Mary Magdalene sits during the song.)

(Hymn: "At the Cross" or song of your choice.)

(Mary Magdalene stands and speaks.)

Overcome by grief, I stood by as Jesus's body was tenderly taken from the cross. I watched as Joseph and Nicodemus placed Him in the new tomb where never a body had lain. The tomb was in a beautiful garden filled with flowers and shrubs. It was indeed a lovely place to lay the body of our Lord. I watched as they wrapped the grave cloths around and around His body, carefully placing the burial napkin over His face.

Oh, but the sun was setting, and the Sabbath was upon us. We had to hurry away before the burial ritual was completed. We women planned to return on the first day of the week to bring more herbs and spices to anoint the body of our Lord. The men pushed the large stone over the mouth of the tomb, and with heavy hearts and broken spirits we left the garden. Our Master was dead. All hope was lost.

(Mary sits during the song.)

(Hymn: "Christ the Lord is Risen Today" or song of your choice.)

(Mary stands and speaks with exuberance.)

Yes, He is risen! He is alive! We women were the first to see

Jesus in the garden near the tomb. We fell down at His feet to worship Him, and He spoke to us, "Do not be afraid," He said. "Go and tell my brothers to go to Galilee; there they will see me."[1]

Oh, yes, He appeared to many of us after His resurrection, and all who saw Him believed. Even Thomas, the one who had doubted, believed after he put his fingers in the nail holes of Jesus's hands and into the wounds on His side. And I testify to you this day that Jesus Christ is the son of God and the Savior of the world. I saw Him crucified, I saw Him buried, and I saw Him resurrected. *Praise God! He lives!* He is the hope of our salvation!

(Mary turns to the cross.)

And what of this cross? This cross so crudely fashioned from two rough pieces of wood. This cross which once held the body of our Savior. "Oh, cross, where is your captive? Oh, death, where is your sting? Oh, grave, where is your victory?"[2] Neither cross nor death nor grave could hold Jesus, for He arose from the dead and ascended into heaven where He now sits at the right hand of God.

And now, as I pass by the cross on the hill, I no longer hide my eyes or turn my face away. The cross is a reminder of how much God loves me—how much God loves us all, sinners though we be. Since that first Easter morn, the cross has taken on a new image for all those who follow Christ. It has become to us a thing of beauty. Christ loved us so much that, on the cross, He sacrificed His life. He paid our ransom and set us free from the chains of sin and death that had bound us since the Garden of Eden.

(Hymn: "The Old Rugged Cross" or other song of your choice. While this song is being sung, members of the congregation come forward. Each person takes a flower from the containers in front and sticks the stem into the

chicken wire on the front and sides of the cross, thus ultimately covering the cross with flowers.)

(Mary stands and delivers her last speech after the congregation is seated.)

Christ's resurrection transformed this cross from a symbol of suffering to a symbol of joy; from a symbol of bitterness to a symbol of hope; from a symbol of death to a symbol of life. The season of Easter is a season of rebirth. Just as the earth, after the death of winter, springs forth with buds and blossoms, so our hearts, after the death of sin, spring forth with new life and fresh beginnings. Behold—the Cross of Easter! The Cross of Promise! The Cross of Salvation!

(Mary sits.)

(End with an appropriate Easter song.)

PRODUCTION NOTES AND RECOMMENDATIONS

Scriptures

Jesus healed Mary from seven demons, she became a follower of Jesus and donated money to His ministry:

Luke 8:1–3

Mary was at the cross when Jesus died:

Matthew 27:45–56; Mark 15:33–41; Luke 23:44–49; John 19:25–27

Mary was there when Jesus was buried:

Matthew 27:57–61; Mark 15:42–47; Luke 23:50–56

Mary was first to see that Jesus had risen from the dead:

Matthew 28:1–7; Mark 16: 1–8; Luke 24:1–10; John 20:1–2

Jesus appeared to Mary after His resurrection:

Matthew 28:8–10: Mark 16:9–11; John 20:10–18

The Musical Drama

This is an Easter production of music and drama for a church service. Mary Magdalene is the only speaker on the stage. She has a speech after each song. The songs and type of music are the choice of the music department; the songs listed in the script are suggestions only. The songs can be performed by soloists, by a traditional choir, or by a praise band with instruments and singers, accompanied by the congregation. Mary enters the stage and stands for her speeches. She has a chair off to the side where she sits during the singing.

The Character

Mary Magdalene was from the seaport town of Magdala, which is a town in Israel. She is mentioned sixteen times by name in the New Testament. In ten of these passages her name heads the list, implying that she occupied a place of prominence among godly women. She is first mentioned in Luke 8:1–3 as the woman from whom Jesus cast seven demons. There is no indication that she was a prostitute as has often been attributed to her. She has been confused with the prostitute in Luke 7:37–38 who washed Jesus's feet with her tears, dried them with her hair, and then anointed them with perfume.

After Jesus healed her, Mary Magdalene became His faithful disciple and followed Him as He ministered. She was at the foot of the cross when Jesus was crucified, she was there when He was buried, and she was the first to see Him after He arose from the dead. I am certain that she was with the gathering of believers who watched as He ascended into heaven fifty days later.

The Character's Relevance to Our Lives

Mary Magdalene was a faithful follower of Jesus. She left everything to follow Jesus, and she gave her own money to support His ministry. The fact that God chose Mary Magdalene as the first person to see the risen Savior lends great credibility to Mary and to Christian women in general. Mary is an example of a woman who gave everything she had to her Lord.

The Flowering of the Cross

A cross large enough to be seen by the congregation should be positioned in the front-middle or to the front-side of the sanctuary. The cross should be covered with chicken wire on three sides. It should be bare at the beginning of the worship service. While the fourth song is being sung, people from the audience will be invited to come down the aisles where there will be several containers of flowers. Each person will take a flower and stick it into the wire. In this way, the cross will soon be covered with beautiful flowers.

Costume

Mary wears a plain robe in a muted color; blue or brown is suggested. She would wear a covering for her head and sandals.

Makeup

Women in Israel at that time, did not wear makeup. However, in a large room and under stage lighting Mary Magdalene's facial features may need to be accentuated. Start with a neutral facial foundation and add mascara and eyeliner to delineate the eyes. A light and natural lip gloss and cheek blush can be added.

Length or Run Time of Drama:

The drama itself is ten to twelve minutes long. This does not include the songs and music or the flowering of the cross.

Mary and Martha of Bethany—Each
Served Jesus in Her Own Way

MARY AND MARTHA OF BETHANY—EACH SERVED JESUS IN HER OWN WAY

A Drama in Two Acts

ACT 1

MARTHA—A WOMAN WHO LOVED TO SERVE

(Martha hurries on-stage with a sense of emergency. She is carrying a basket of fruit. She looks off-stage for Mary and calls out.)

Mary! Mary! Oh, where can she be?

(Martha sets the fruit basket on the table and addresses the audience.)

Jesus and the twelve are at the city gates and are on their way here now. There is so much to be done! This fruit needs to be arranged on the table. The fire must be watched because the lamb must be roasted to perfection. I want the meat to be perfect—nicely browned, juicy and moist, well cooked, but not dry. Our best wine and olives must be ready to serve.

(Martha sits in the chair behind the table and picks up a bowl of bread dough)

This bread must be baked, and it must be watched. It must be golden brown and not burned. Let me see--what else? Oh yes, my best coverlet must be placed on the bed where Jesus will sleep. I want the best of everything for Jesus.

I have my reputation to uphold as the finest hostess in Bethany. My meals are perfect because I work so hard to make them so. My house is spotless, with not a speck of dust anywhere. I am busy from morning till night. The fine hospitality of Martha of Bethany is known far and wide.

(Martha rises and looks to the side of stage.)

I hear voices in the outer room. **(She listens for three seconds.)** Lazarus is welcoming Jesus and His friends.

(Martha continues to look off-stage, with hands on hips and elbows outward.)

And there's Mary, running right in to sit at Jesus's feet. She's going to enjoy herself while I do all the work. **(Martha turns back to the audience.)** She does this every time He comes. I love Jesus as much as she does. I too would love to sit at His feet and listen to Him speak, but someone has to be responsible to get things done. And that someone is always me!

(Martha sits. She picks up a jar and pours a little flour on the raw dough and begins to knead the bread with vigor).

On one occasion I complained to Jesus. I said, "Lord, don't you care that my sister has left me to do the work by myself. Tell her to help me."[1]

Then He took my hand in His and said quite lovingly, "Martha, Martha, you are worried and upset about many things, but only one thing is needed. Mary has chosen what is better and it will not be taken away from her."[2]

(Martha repeats Jesus's words rather begrudgingly.)

Mary has chosen what is better. Sometimes I don't think Jesus understands. I'm so busy because I'm doing all these things for Him. If I only had more time and If I knew when He was coming, I could be prepared! Then I too could be sitting at His feet. But how can I possibly get everything ready at the last minute!

(Martha remains seated and stops kneading as she tells her story.)

Take the time when my brother Lazarus was so sick. He was sick unto death. Mary and I nursed him night and day, but he grew worse. We knew of Jesus's power to heal, so I sent a messenger to Jesus saying, "Lord, the one you love is sick."[3]

Day after day went by. Lazarus grew worse, and Jesus didn't come. Then our greatest nightmare was realized—our little brother died. Oh, how we mourned. How we wailed and wept. We loved our brother. I had been like a mother to him. I knew that Jesus loved Lazarus too, so why, why hadn't He come to heal him? Lazarus was dead and in the tomb four days when at last Jesus appeared.

I was terribly upset when I went out to meet Him and I said, "Lord, if you had been here my brother would not have died. But I know that even now God will give you whatever you ask."[4]

Jesus said, "Your brother will rise again."[5]

I answered, "I know he will rise again in the resurrection at the last day"[6]

Then Jesus said to me, "I am the resurrection and the life. He who believes in me will live, even though he dies, and whoever lives and believes in me will never die. Do you believe this?"[7]

"Yes, Lord," I replied. "I believe that you are the Christ, the Son of God, who was to come into the world."[8]

I ran home and told Mary that Jesus was here and was asking for her. She rose up and ran to Him, and many Jews who were in the house followed her. When she reached Jesus, she fell at His feet and cried, "Lord if you had been here, my brother would not have died."[9]

When Jesus saw Mary and her friends weeping, He was deeply moved, and Jesus also wept. Then Jesus went to the tomb and said, "Take away the stone."[10]

But I protested, "Lord, by this time there is a bad odor, for he has been there four days."[11]

Jesus replied, "Did I not tell you that if you believed, you would see the glory of God?"[12]

So, the men took away the stone. Then Jesus looked up and said, "Father I thank you that you have heard me. I knew that you always hear me, but I said this for the benefit of the people standing here, that they may believe that you sent me."[13] When He had said this, Jesus called in a loud voice, "Lazarus, come out!"[14]

And—miracle of miracles—my brother, Lazarus, came out, his hands and feet wrapped with strips of linen and a cloth around his face. Jesus said to them, "Take off the grave cloths and let him go."[15]

They did! And Lazarus stood before us alive and well, strong and healthy. I ran to him and embraced him. And many of the Jews who were there that day believed that Jesus was the Son of God.

I invited everyone to my home that day for a great feast. How happy we were. And now Jesus is with us once again. Oh, what a celebration this will be.

(Martha puts her hands to her face and gasps.)

Oh my, I forgot to check on the roasting meat! And I must get this bread into the oven.

(Martha picks up the bread dough she has been kneading and hurries off the stage, calling for Mary.) "Mary, come quickly. I need your help!"

End of Act 1

MARY AND MARTHA OF BETHANY—EACH SERVED JESUS IN HER OWN WAY

ACT 2

MARY OF BETHANY—THE WOMAN WHO MADE THE BEST CHOICE

(Mary enters with enthusiasm and places a container of precious ointment at the front of the table, facing the audience.)

Please don't think that I am lazy. I want to help my sister, Martha. And I don't want the bread to burn. It's just that I want to spend every moment with my Lord Jesus. He teaches us that His words are the bread of life.

I believe that Jesus is God—God who has come down to us in the flesh. I have believed this ever since He raised our brother, Lazarus, from the dead. I want to be with Him at every opportunity. I want to listen to His every word and understand all of His teaching.

Have you noticed that Jesus speaks freely to women, and in

public at that? Jesus has told me that God our Father loves me in the same way in which He loves my brother Lazarus. As a woman, I have never dared dream of such love. This knowledge has given me a great freedom of spirit.

Since I have met Jesus, I am no longer ashamed of being born a woman. I have learned from Him that God looks upon the heart of a person and that we are all—men and women—created in the image of God and equal in His sight. And that in God's kingdom, there is no male or female.

Jesus allows me, a woman, to sit at His feet along with the men and listen as He speaks. The Pharisees criticize Him for eating with women and sinners. They speak openly against Him. The chief priest hates Him because so many Jews are following Him, especially after He raised my brother, Lazarus, from the dead.

I have been trying to think of some way to honor Jesus and show Him how much He means to me. I am eternally grateful to Jesus for the life of my brother, Lazarus. I can never repay Him. Martha honors Him by the delicious meals she prepares, her hospitality, and the comforts of this home where He and His friends can relax and rest.

But I have nothing to offer Him except my love and devotion and this precious ointment.

(Mary picks up the container of ointment from the table.)

It is very expensive. This costly perfume is worth an entire year's wages. I have saved it for quite some time. I have saved it for a special occasion. This perfume is also used to anoint the body for burial.

(She delivers the next sentence in a stage whisper.)

I have heard that there are those priests and Pharisees who hate Jesus so much that they may plot to kill Him! **(She grimaces**

in pain.) Maybe I should save this perfume for His burial. Oh, I shudder to think such thoughts.

(Mary places the perfume on the table and sits in the chair beside the table.)

I had no purpose in life until I met Jesus. I was like a ship without a rudder; like a sheep without a shepherd. Oh, I lacked for nothing. I had a comfortable home, many possessions, and an abundance of food and livestock. I was faithful to the Law of Moses, but something was missing. Then I met Jesus. I heard Him speak, and I saw His miracles. I, along with Martha and Lazarus, recognized Him as the Messiah.

We became close friends, and He made our home His resting place when He was near. And then—as unbelievable as it may sound—after our brother Lazarus had lain four days in the tomb, Jesus raised him from the dead. I saw it with my own eyes. How could I not believe that Jesus was the Son of God?

Since that time, praise God, I have been able to give my life completely and unconditionally to Jesus. That is why, when He is here, I can think of nothing else but sitting at His feet and listening to His every word. Just being in His presence brings such blessings. Wouldn't you do the same? But Martha cannot understand me, and I cannot understand her! She loves Jesus and she saw the miracle, yet she is not able to put Him first in everything. She always seems too busy for Jesus.

I have learned from Jesus, that unless I put Him first in my life, I will never find that purpose for which I was created, and my life will never be complete. I will flounder and stumble through my days searching for peace, contentment, and fulfillment. Jesus calls us to put Him first—first in our thoughts, our minds, our hearts; first in our family, our home, our time. Oh Martha, Martha, why can't you yield yourself completely to our Lord? Why can't you give up and let Jesus take control?

(Mary pauses and looks away for a moment. She then turns to the audience and speaks with determination.)

I've made up my mind. I know that I will be criticized, but I'm going into the next room where Jesus is reclining and pour this precious perfume on His feet and then wipe His feet with my hair. Nothing is too precious or expensive for the feet of my Lord.

(Mary looks at the audience with a new idea in her mind and a smile on her face as she invites them to accompany her into the presence of Jesus.)

Will you not come with me? You, too, can sit at Jesus's feet. Please come with me into the presence of Jesus.

(Mary speaks slowly as she leads the audience into a mental encounter with Jesus. She pauses often, giving them time to visualize themselves in each scene.)

I invite you to bow your head and close your eyes. Now, picture yourself sitting at Jesus's feet. **(She pauses to a count of five.)** Join me as I anoint His feet with my most precious gift. **(She pauses to a count of five.)** I invite you to anoint Him with your most precious gifts: the gift of your love, the gift of your obedience, the gift of your surrender, the gift of your life. **(She pauses to a count of ten.)** Now look up into His face and see His eyes of love smiling down at you. **(She pauses to a count of five.)**

Keep looking into His eyes and silently say to Him, "I give myself to you, Jesus—wholly and unconditionally." **(She pauses to a count of five.)** "Jesus, I put you first in everything. I invite you to be Lord of my heart and King of my life." **(She pauses to a count of five.)**

As you look into His eyes, you see His love as He looks back at you—an undying love that existed before the creation of the world, a love that will live on into eternity. Jesus died for you on the cross, and by His stripes you are healed. By His blood you are cleansed as white as snow. By His death you are reconciled and redeemed. By His resurrection you have the promise of eternal life.

And now, feel Jesus place His hands upon your head as He gives you His blessing. **(She pauses to a count of five.)** Feel the warmth of His hands upon your head. **(She pauses to a count of five.)** Feel the Holy Spirit flowing from His hands into you and through you, filling you up and coming to rest and reside in your heart. Hear Jesus say that He will live in your heart as long as you open it to Him. **(She pauses to a count of five.)**

Let us pray: Dear Lord, we strive to put You first in everything we do. We give ourselves to You, Jesus. We anoint Your feet with the perfume of our surrendered lives. Let us love to serve You as Martha did. Let us never forget to sit at Your feet and abide in You as Mary did. Help us to spend time sitting at Your feet in prayer and in Your Word. Please accept our gifts and purify our hearts. Let us never forget that it is not by our works, but by Your grace that we are saved. In Your precious name we pray. Amen

(Mary stands, bows to the audience.)

And now I bid you shalom!

(She smiles and exits the stage leaving the spice container on the table.)

End of drama.

Production Notes and Recommendations

Scriptures

Luke 10:38–42; John 11:1–47; John 12:1–11

The monologues of Martha and Mary, performed as one program, are powerful. They can be performed by one person or by two people. Each monologue is approximately ten to fifteen minutes long, and there should be a five-minute pause between Acts 1 and 2. The program is a twenty-five- to thirty-minute production. Fill the five-minute pause between acts with a soloist or a hymn sung by the audience. This is not an intermission. You do not want to lose momentum.

The Characters

Martha is the older sister; Mary is the middle sister; and Lazarus is the younger brother. The passage in Luke 10:38 suggests that the home belonged to Martha. Martha "opens her home" to Jesus and seems to be in charge. Martha is known as an excellent cook and hostess. She is the epitome of a meticulous person and a fretful worrier who is concerned more with things rather than people.

Mary, on the other hand, is more concerned with spiritual matters. It is Mary who sits listening to Jesus speak rather than helping Martha in the kitchen. Lazarus is not portrayed in this drama; however, the story revolves in part around him.

The Characters' Relevance to Our Lives Today

Books have been written and Bible studies produced on the lives of Martha and Mary. What can we learn from Martha:

- We must examine the distractions and activities in our lives that can pull us away from our Lord.
- We must prioritize our time so that we too can sit at Jesus's feet—studying the scriptures, praying, giving thanks, singing, and worshiping.
- We must get our priorities and our focus right in the sight of God.
- We must not measure our service to God by the actions of others or compare ourselves to others.
- We must not be critical of others who may worship and serve Jesus in a different way than we do.

What can we learn from Mary:

- We must have a servant's heart.
- We must give everything to Jesus: all that we are and all that we possess.
- We must put Him first in our lives.
- We must believe His Word, have faith in Him, and trust Him.
- We must have no fear as we openly worship Him.
- We must realize, as Mary did, that Jesus sets us free.
- We must anoint His feet with the perfume of our lives.

If we combine the attributes of these two godly women, we will put Jesus first and thereby be able to lead a life of *service* that is motived by *love*. We each have a position to fill and a job to do in the Kingdom of God. All we need to do is simply say, "Send me, Lord, to do whatever it is you require of me." We each have our own God-given gifts to use in service to Him. Let us never envy or belittle the gifts of others; rather, let us love and encourage each other as God loves and encourages us.

Stage Direction

Martha is agitated as she enters the stage carrying a shallow basket of fruit. The fruit can be real or artificial. During her first speech, she sets the basket on the table. Martha is upset and worried because Jesus and His disciples are not far from her house, and the feast is not yet ready. She is upset with Mary who wants to spend her time with Jesus instead of helping her with the food preparation. As Martha voices her concerns, she sits behind the table and begins kneading the lump of bread dough. A can of biscuit dough can be used. Just mix all of the biscuits from the can into one lump of dough to be kneaded. Don't forget to sprinkle flour on the dough as you knead so the dough doesn't stick to your hands. Martha accentuates her frustration with Mary as she vigorously kneads the bread dough!

Mary, on the other hand, enters with a smile on her face and carries a decorative jar or bottle that represents a container filled with expensive ointment. As she begins to speak, she sets the container on the front part of the table. Mary speaks in a friendly, easy manner. She is happy because Jesus is coming to their home, and she can't wait to sit at His feet and listen to His teachings. She wants to help Martha, but her desire to sit in the presence of Jesus is more important to her. Mary picks up the ointment when she begins explaining its purpose. She then sits on the chair or stool that is positioned beside the table.

At the end of Mary's drama, she leads the audience through a meditation. Mary must deliver this section very slowly, allowing the audience enough time to visualize and experience what she is telling them. Throughout the meditation you will see stage directions telling Mary to pause for five or ten counts. It is particularly important that Mary pauses to allow time for this visualization to happen. Mary can have a copy of the meditation lying on the table. Without picking it up, she may read from it, since the audience will have their heads bowed and eyes closed.

Biblical Setting

This event in the life of Jesus occurred in the town of Bethany, which is a short distance from Jerusalem. Martha, her sister Mary, and their brother Lazarus shared a deep love for Jesus, who, with His disciples, stayed in their home whenever they were in the region. On this occasion, Martha has prepared a dinner for Jesus and His followers. The dinner occurred during the Jewish Passover, the day before Jesus's triumphal entry into Jerusalem.

Stage Setting

Use the same stage setting for both dramas. One table is positioned at center stage, covered with a cream-colored or earth-tone cloth that reaches the floor, hiding the legs. A card table is perfect.

One simple wooden chair or stool is behind the table, and another chair or stool is beside the table. Both chairs or stools should face the audience.

Properties (Props)

One basket is filled with fresh or artificial fruit; Martha carries it as she enters. One shallow wood or pottery bowl or platter contains a mound of raw bread dough. It sets on the table. A small pottery jar, bowl, or vase containing flour is on the table. Martha sprinkles some on her hands and on the dough when she is kneading (otherwise the dough will stick to her hands). Other items of interest can be on the table if you wish: small pottery vase of flowers, candle, or small bowl.

A small to medium jar or bottle is carried in by Mary. It represents the container of expensive perfume with which she plans to anoint the feet of Jesus. The script for Mary's creative visualization can be on the table adjacent to the chair where she will sit, unobservable by the audience.

Costumes

For One Woman Performing Both Characters

Martha would wear a basic loose robe and sandals. Her hair should be covered with some type of scarf or shawl. When performing Mary, she would wear a cloak over the same dress and wear a different headdress and the same sandals.

For Two Women Performing

Martha and Mary each wear a long robe and head coverings. A cloak would be optional for either of them. See Production Ideas for additional details on costumes.

Makeup

Hebrew women of that day wore no makeup. If the room is small, no makeup is needed other than a light lip coloring and a neutral facial foundation. However, in a large room and under stage lighting, the facial features may need to be accentuated. You might add mascara and eyeliner to delineate the eyes. A light and natural lip gloss and cheek blush can be added.

Length or Run Time of Monologue

This program is twenty-five to thirty minutes long. Each monologue is twelve to fifteen minutes long, depending on pauses and delivery of each actress. Add five minutes between acts, which can be filled by a song performed by a solo or sung by the audience.

ENDNOTES

Chapter 1: Eve—Mother of All Living

1   Genesis 3:15
2   Genesis 4:1

Chapter 2: Ruth and Naomi—Whither Thou Goest I will Go

Naomi—Call Me Mara

1   Ruth 1:8–9
2   Ruth 1:10
3   Ruth 1:15
4   Ruth 1:16–17
5   Ruth 1:19
6   Ruth 1:20–21
7   Psalm 30:11–12

Ruth—Your God Shall be My God

1   Ruth 1:16b
2   Ruth 2:20
3   Ruth 3:1–4
4   Ruth 3:9a
5   Ruth 3:9b
6   Ruth 3:10–13
7   Ruth 3:14
8   Ruth 4:3–4

9   Ruth 4:9-10
10 Ruth 4:14–15
11 Ruth 4:17
12 Psalm 108:3–5

Chapter 3: Hannah—The Praying Woman

1   1 Samuel 1:11
2   1 Samuel 1:14
3   1 Samuel 1:15–16
4   1 Samuel 1:17
5   1 Samuel 1:18
6   Samuel sounds like the Hebrew word for "heard of God."
7   1 Samuel 2:1–2 Has been called, "Hannah's Magnificat"
8   Psalm 40:1–3

Chapter 4: Queen Esther—For Such a Time as This

1   Esther 3:11
2   Esther 4:11
3   Esther 4:12–14
4   Esther 4:15–16
5   Esther 5:3
6   Esther 5:4
7   Esther 5:14
8   Esther 6:3b
9   Esther 6:6
10 Esther 6:9b
11 Esther 6:10
12 Esther 7:3–4
13 Esther 7:5
14 Esther 7:6
15 Esther 7:8b
16 Purim: Begins on the evening of March 9 and ends on the evening of March 10. Purim is pronounced poo-REEM in Eastern tradition and PUH-rim in Western tradition.

Chapter 5: Lady Wisdom—Listen to My Voice

1 Proverbs 8:6–7; 10–13
2 Proverbs 8:22–36
3 Proverbs 1:7
4 Proverbs 3:5–6
5 Matthew 12:42b
6 1 Corinthians 1:18–31; 2:1–16 (Christ is the Wisdom of God)
7 Proverbs 3:13–18

Chapter 6: Mary of Nazareth—Mother of Jesus

1 Luke 1:28
2 Luke 1:30
3 Luke 1:34
4 Luke 1:35–37
5 Luke 1:38
6 Luke 1:42–45
7 Luke 1:46–49
8 Matthew 1:20–21
9 Isaiah 7:14
10 Luke 2:14
11 Luke 2:34–35
12 Matthew 2:13
13 Luke 2:48
14 Luke 2:49
15 Luke 2:52

Chapter 7: Mary Magdalene—In the Garden

1 Luke 8:2
2 Luke 8:1–3
3 Matthew 19:14
4 Acts 10:41
5 Mark 11:9–10
6 John 20:2
7 John 20:13
8 John 20:15

9   John 20:15
10 John 20:16
11 John 20:16
12 John 20:17
13 John 20:18

Chapter 8: Mary Magdalene—He Is Risen

1   Mark 11:9–10
2   John 20:2
3   John 20:13
4   John 20:15
5   John 20:15
6   John 20:16
7   John 20:16
8   John 20:17
9   John 20:18

Chapter 9: The Easter Miracle—As Told by Mary Magdalene

1   Matthew 28:10
2   Hosea 13:14, 1 Corinthians 15:55–56

Chapter 10: Martha and Mary—Served Jesus Each in Her Own Way

1   Luke 10:40
2   Luke 10:41
3   John 11:3
4   John 11:21–22
5   John 11:23
6   John 11:24
7   John 11:25–26
8   John 11:27
9   John 11:32
10 John 11:39
11 John 11:39

12 John 11:40
13 John 11:41–42
14 John 11:43
15 John 11:44

CPSIA information can be obtained
at www.ICGtesting.com
Printed in the USA
FSHW011950271021
85801FS